EMPOWERING PROGRESS

LEON DRENNAN

Additional books by Leon Drennan:

The Power of Purpose and Priorities – Leading the Way
People – Your Grestest Asset or Biggest Headache
Seasons of the Soul – Which one are you in?
Good King / Bad King – Which One Are You?

EMPOWERING PROGRESS

LEON DRENNAN

Vision Leadership Foundation
Brentwood, TN

Empowering Progress by Leon Drennan
Published by Vision Leadership Foundation, Brentwood, TN 37027
©Copyright 2016 Vision Leadership Foundation. All Rights Reserved.

Any form of duplication—physical, digital, photographic or otherwise is expressly forbidden, unless authorized in writing by the author/publisher.

ISBN 978-0-9904033-8-8

Scripture quoted in this book comes from one of the four sources noted below. Unless otherwise noted, the default version for use is the New American Standard Bible.

Scripture taken from THE HOLY BIBLE, ENGLISH STANDARD VERSION® (ESV®) Copyright © 2001 by Crossway, a publishing ministry of Good News Publishers. Used by permission. All rights reserved.

Scripture taken from the KING JAMES VERSION, public domain.

Scripture taken from the NEW AMERICAN STANDARD BIBLE®, Copyright © 1960, 1962, 1963, 1968, 1971, 1972, 1973, 1975, 1977, 1995 by The Lockman Foundation. Used by permission.

Scripture taken from THE HOLY BIBLE, NEW INTERNATIONAL VERSION®, NIV® Copyright © 1973, 1978, 1984, 2011 by Biblica, Inc.® Used by permission. All rights reserved worldwide.

The contents of this book are based on my recollection and understanding of Scripture as inspired by the Spirit and by a lifetime of leadership experience in a large, complex organization, as well as on the observation of others in leadership roles. My thoughts have been influenced by some great books and Christian authors as referenced in this book. Any perceived similarities to leadership or management materials in the marketplace are coincidental except those which I have specifically cited. — Leon Drennan, Vision Leadership Foundation

Dedication

This book is dedicated in loving memory of my mom and dad, who taught me to work hard, persevere, and pursue God. Also, to my children Scott, Allyson, and Kelsey—in birth order. They bring me great joy and gave me three good reasons to persevere. Finally, and most importantly, to my wife Debbie, who has loved me unconditionally for thirty-eight years and who has persevered with me.

Acknowledgments

I appreciate the Frist family and all the leaders at HCA, too many to mention by name, who allowed me to serve and learn in a great organization for thirty-one years. I especially thank Dr. Frist Jr. for his great example of using power for good. I thank Diana Rush, my executive assistant of many years and trusted friend, who worked a fulltime job and helped in her spare time with formatting and graphics in this book. Additionally, I thank all my past colleagues, employees, peers, and associates for the fun we had together, what I learned from them, what we accomplished together, and, most importantly, for their friendship.

Also, a big thank you to Scott Drennan and Darrel Girardier for their inspiring work and design of the book cover. A special thanks goes to Fred MacKrell at AuthorTrack.com, who guided me in every major phase of this project and enhanced the graphics and layout of the book with his creativity.

Thanks to David Roach for his great editing skills.

Empowering Progress

Table of Contents

Preface ix
Introduction xi

Part I   **Progress** 1
Chapter 1   Planning 3
Chapter 2   You Can't Make Progress "Fighting Fires" 15
Chapter 3   Leading Change 29
Chapter 4   Progress Through Documentation and Training 47
Chapter 5   Progress Through Enabling Control Systems 51
Chapter 6   Progress Through Measurement 61

Part II   **Power** 69
Chapter 7   Abusing Power 73
Chapter 8   A Model Sure To Fail—Micro-Managing 81
Chapter 9   What Is Real Power? 87
Chapter 10   How To Become A Leader 95
Chapter 11   Power of the Position vs. Power of Service 101
Chapter 12   The Approach To Power—Keep It or Distribute It? 107
Chapter 13   Empowerment Through Effective Delegation 119
Chapter 14   Empowerment Through High Expectations 133
Chapter 15   Conclusion 139
                     Endnotes 145

Notes

Preface

I've always been fascinated with people, leadership, and organizations. I learned about these through growing up on the family farm, hauling hay as a teenager, working in a factory, working in a rock quarry during my college years, serving for over thirty-five years in business, church, and nonprofit organizations, and studying the leadership of kings in the Old Testament and Jesus in the New Testament.

I realized as a young man that my calling and passion was to develop leaders and help improve organizations. I worked for thirty-one years at Hospital Corporation of America (HCA), the largest for-profit hospital company in the world. I was blessed with the opportunity to lead in a variety of executive roles, which allowed me to lead auditors, construction and engineering professionals, nurses, doctors, and others. I served my last twelve years as president of HCA Physician Services.

My calling and passion never changed, though I wore many different hats and worked with people in many different professions. I loved developing people and building, redefining, and improving organizations. Although my division was maturing and growing fast when I led Physician Services, I started sensing God's leading to make a move. I swallowed hard and, in faith, started making plans to leave the company where I had spent most of my adult life. It was one of the hardest things I've ever done. My transition took a couple of years before I left HCA and was ready for the next phase of life.

Empowering Progress

I formed Vision Leadership Foundation in 2010 with a goal to mentor, coach, and train leaders using what God has taught me through many years and varied experiences. This phase of life involves developing leaders and helping organizations function better in the business, nonprofit, and ministry sectors. The goal is to help leaders:

- Get more done in less time and with less frustration and stress.

- Create more profitability (if they are business owners) so they have more financial resources to contribute to ministries and charities.

- Have more time for their spouses, children, churches, communities, friends, and enjoyment of life.

- Create healthy organizational cultures to benefit their employees rather than bringing difficulty and stress into their lives.

I have a growing desire to be able to give more to ministries and charities. I believe that through helping others, I can do more for ministries and charities than I would have ever been able to do myself.

Introduction

Early in my career, I worked with a lot of young professionals. One thing they always wanted to know was how to get promoted or get ahead. It's not an unusual question. In fact, it's basic for all people. Part of what we dream about for our children is for them to have a better life than we have. The reason people want to come to America is to have a better life than they would in their countries of origin. The need for progress seems innate.

I think it was put there by God because He expects us to make progress. Look at the parable of the talents. The master condemned one man for burying his talent and not making progress. He commended the other two men for taking their talents and doubling them. In the creation story in Genesis, God established order and then caused His creation to flourish. If we are going to carry on with God's work, then we also must bring order to chaos and cause things to flourish. Especially in leadership roles, we aim create order and cause the people in our organizations, as well as those the organization touches, to flourish.

This book explains how to make that happen. From my experience, I have learned there are several steps to making continual progress. It's impossible to make maximum progress if you leave out any one of the steps. Also, I've learned the hard way that you can't do it by yourself. You will only have a flourishing organization if you know how to properly empower others. That's why the title of the book is *Empowering Progress*.

In part one, we discuss the key elements to making progress. First, we seek God through prayer to get His leadership. Then we create a plan. Studies have shown that people who create plans—in fact, multiple iterations of plans—have the most success. God had a plan for His creation. It didn't just happen. He knew the end from the very beginning. Good leaders plan.

Next, leaders lead change. Change is difficult, and many avoid it. Yet to make progress, you can't stay where you are. Part of leading change is avoiding costly mistakes that take you backward instead of forward.

As the organization grows, you will need to introduce higher levels of documentation and training to help people function at their optimal levels. Good documentation allows you to maintain consistent procedures even when employee turnover occurs. It also makes it easier for each successive generation of employees to build on the progress of previous employees. Good training helps create consistency among the employees.

You also need to introduce reporting mechanisms to help you know the status of initiatives, keep people on track, and give them early warnings when they are off-track.

Finally, you will need to establish key measures and feedback mechanisms so people know how they're doing. If you doubt the need to make progress, just think about this: would you play any kind of sport if they didn't keep score so that you knew how you were doing?

The second part of the book is about the use of power. To position your team to make progress, you will need to use power properly and know how to empower people. Most people misuse power some or even most of their life. I share with you how I misused power and observed others do so.

Leaders either try to serve people through their positions of power or they try to manipulate, control, and use people. An overreaching need to control causes leaders to become less effective because they develop patterns of micromanaging. There is a difference between managers and real leaders as well as between real power and temporary power. You distribute power through effective organization and good delegation techniques. Finally, high expectations play a key role in empowering others.

Along the way, at times I will refer to the DISC personality profile system. It is a commonly used personality profile that categories people based on four major categories of behavior: dominance, influence, steadiness, and compliance. The dominant personality likes to be responsible for a project. The influencing personality likes to market and sell the project. The steady, or compliant, personality does a great deal of the work and appreciates order.

Amid my first real challenge as a young leader, I discovered a couple of important things. One was that you need to understand the personality profiles of your team, as well as your own, in order to know what inspires them and what turns them off. Next, I learned that sharing the power and engaging the team in the planning and visioning process will help you avoid the near mutiny I experienced the first time I tried to lead like an autocratic manager. My hope is that by reading this book, you'll learn how to face leadership challenges more effectively than I did.

Notes

Part I

I. PROGRESS

"A wise man will hear and increase in learning, and a man of understanding will acquire wise counsel."
Proverbs 1:4-6

"Without consultation, plans are frustrated, but with many counselors they succeed."
Proverbs 15:22

"Where there is no guidance the people fall, but in abundance of counselors there is victory."
Proverbs 11:14

"When the apostles returned, they gave an account to Him of all they had done."
Luke 9:10

"So then each one of us will give an account of himself to God."
Romans 14:12

Questions to Ponder

- Do you find yourself always fighting fires?

- Are you always "swinging for the fences," trying to hit a grand slam in your organization?

- Would you be content and relieved to have steady, reliable progress in your organization without the significant ups and downs?

- Do your people receive reports on how they and the organization are doing at regular intervals?

Issues Covered in this Section

- The importance of proper planning.

- Leading change effectively.

- The importance of documentation and training.

- The components and value of control systems.

- The value of the measurement and feedback.

INTRODUCTION TO PROGRESS

Everybody wants to make progress. One of the primary questions people ask in organizations is: How can I get ahead here? What parent doesn't want a better life for their children?

When God created this world, first He gave it form. Then He caused it to flourish. His first command to us was to be fruitful and multiply. In other words, to make progress. The parable of the talents in the New Testament reiterates this. The stewards who took what the owner entrusted to them and multiplied it were commended while the person who buried the talent was condemned. We are expected by our Creator to make progress, and the need for progress is built within us.

In this first section of the book we talk about progress.

Notes

Chapter 1

PLANNING

> **Thought:**
> If you don't know where you are going,
> any path will take you there.
> Do you strongly desire progress, but have no plan for it?

*"Declaring the end from the beginning, and from ancient times
the things which have not been done, saying,
'My purpose will be established,
and I will accomplish all my good pleasure'."*

Isaiah 46:10

> *"Your eyes have seen my unformed substance;
> and in your book were written all the days that were dreamed for
> me, when as yet there was not one of them."*
>
> *Psalm 139:16*

You are not going to create positive change without a plan. God planned everything before He created anything. Scripture says He knew your days before there was one of them (Psalms 139:16). One of the best examples I can think of to illustrate an effective planning process is found in the book of Nehemiah in the Old Testament. Nehemiah got every aspect of the planning process right. Outlined in this chapter is the process he used. It worked for him. And when I have had the presence of mind to follow the same process, it has worked for me.

Nehemiah illustrates the planning and process needed to make progress.

Key Components in the Planning Process

The Nehemiah Model

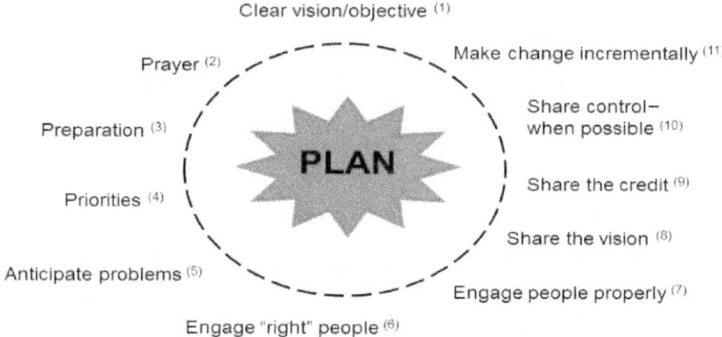

Chapter 1 – Planning

Supporting Scripture

(1) Nehemiah 2:5 — rebuild the wall
(2) Nehemiah 1:4-6
(3) Nehemiah 2:6-7, 11-15
(4) Matthew 6:33
(5) Nehemiah 2:7-9; 4:11-19
(6) Kings 12:6-12
(7) Ephesians 4:8-11
(8) Nehemiah 2:17-18
(9) Proverbs 25:6
(10) Revelation 3:20
(11) Nehemiah, Chapter 3

Vision | Problem/Opportunity

We see that Nehemiah's planning process started with a burden or a problem and an opportunity.

"They said to me, the remnant there in the providence who survived captivity are in great distress and reproach, and the wall of Jerusalem was broken down and its gates are burned with fire."

Nehemiah 1: 3

The passion in people rises when something makes them mad, glad, or sad.[1] We are glad when we see a great opportunity and thus begin planning to capitalize on it. In Nehemiah's case, he was sad and God revealed to him an opportunity to do something about the situation.

Prayer

Nehemiah 1:4-6, says he "sat down and wept and mourned for days; and was fasting and praying before the God of heaven." In his prayer time, he got perfectly aligned with God. He confessed his own sins and those of his people. Then he was prepared to hear God's plan for him. Regardless of religious affiliation or spiritual background, most people pray. Usually, it's not *if* they pray; it's simply when and how they pray. Most people tend to get in a jam following their own plans and then begin to pray asking God to help them out.

Then there are those who think they are being spiritual by praying earlier in the process. The problem is they have already made up their minds and then simply are praying for God to bless their plans. That's not how Nehemiah prayed. He had a burden after hearing what had happened to his home city of Jerusalem and took his burden before the Lord.

Prayer is where God reveals His plan to us. We like to talk about vision in organizational life. For the Christian, vision is really God's revelation of His plan and our involvement. Nehemiah had a vision for rebuilding the wall in Jerusalem, but that plan came from God. Nehemiah was simply to have a leadership role in it. He was clear about the vision, his role in it, and God's alignment with it before he did anything else.

Preparation

Nehemiah thought and made preparations for what would be required next and for the questions that would be asked of him. Prayer was also part of his preparation. In Nehemiah 1:11, he prayed that God would give the king compassion to help him. Let's not take lightly the prayer time of Nehemiah as he prepared. People who served the king in that day and were sad in the presence of the king were subject to dismissal from their role or even death for being unhappy around the king. Nehemiah prayed for the king's favor and showed his sadness in Nehemiah 2:1-2: "Now I had not been sad in his presence." So they said to me, 'Why is your face sad though you are not sick? This is nothing but sadness of heart.'" Nehemiah told him why. The king said to him, "What would you request?" This is where preparation in prayer and good administrative thinking came in. Nehemiah said, "If it please the King, and if your servant has found favor before you, send me to Judah, to the city of my father's tombs, that I may rebuild it." The king asked, "How long will your journey be, and when will you return?" So it pleased the king to send him, and he gave the king a definite time. There was a lot involved in rebuilding the walls in Jerusalem. Nehemiah must have spent hours thinking and figuring how long this massive endeavor would take. Therefore, when asked, he had a sure and ready answer.

I have seen leaders make many mistakes in this area over the years. And I made my share as well. The first mistake is not being able to answer basic questions about the cost and timeline when you're asking permission to do a big project. Another mistake is under-resourcing a project. There is a tendency to want to lowball the cost and time required to increase the chances of getting approval for a project. This usually comes back to bite you in the end when you have to go back and ask for more resources. It's harder to get them after you miss your initial estimates and don't live up to your commitments.

I think the biggest single mistake I see people make in organizational life is the tendency to systemically over-promise and under-deliver. We had an initiative in Physician Services once where we had started small and spread the initiative through several hospitals and divisions. The concept had been sufficiently tested and proven, so we were asking the CEO for funding to expand the initiative. We had worked for weeks on the business plan, and the team anticipated a $200 million measurable benefit over five years to the company. I looked at the business plans and thought the results were achievable if everything went right. But there was not much margin for error, and some of the results were based on what I considered soft measures. I asked the team to cut the measurable benefit in the projections to $100 million. The team asked me why. I said, "Let's think through this. If we promise $200 million in benefits and deliver $150 million, are you going to get an 'atta boy' for the $150 million or criticized for the $50 million miss? By contrast, if we promise a $100 million benefit and deliver $150 million in benefit, how do you think that will be received? Which position would you prefer to be in?" The team got the point and quickly agreed to make the changes.

The discussion didn't end there though. I explained there was more to my thinking. If I let the discussion stop there, they might have been left with the impression that the goal on an initiative is to "sandbag" the results. That wasn't my intent at all. I brought up several things that could happen and would be barriers to the $200 million projection and asked if we had contingency plans to fill gaps. I asked if anybody thought the soft numbers in the projections would be attacked by some of the senior executives in the boardroom when we went for approval. Scripture tells us to "build on the solid rock" (Matthew 7:24-27). I know the Scriptures are talking about building something solid spiritually. But I think there is a practical application of that spiritual principle. Build on what is solid.

I've seen many times people going to meetings with seven justifications for a project.

The first four are rock solid and what I call "no-brainers." The last three are potential benefits but more questionable, with the last one being a bit of a stretch. Rather than going for the easy win, putting the four concrete justifications out and stopping at that for approval, I've seen many employees lose or delay approval of their proposals by listing of less concrete benefits and provoking discussion and debate. I counseled the team to build on what was rock solid so that we did not risk losing credibility over things that could be seen by others as a bit of a stretch, even if we believed we were right.

You remember the principle from Scripture of "going the extra mile." This is where Jesus taught people to do more than what they were required by law to do. An extension of this foundational principle is doing more than what you promised to do. People who systemically over-promise and under-deliver are not seen as trustworthy, even though they may deliver some substantial results over time.

When we got the boardroom on this initiative, the team was well prepared, and it went much as we had anticipated. After substantial discussion, with people trying to poke holes in the projections without success, the company CEO asked a question: "Leon, how sure are you about this $100 million in benefits?" Because the team had prepared so well and we had only left in the projections what we knew was solid, I was able to look him in the eye and say with a great deal of confidence, "I have a 95% confidence level in that number and the fact it is likely conservative. How many times in the past have I told you we could do something that we didn't deliver on or exceed?" He said, "$100 million over five years is enough for me. Does anybody else have any questions?" Of course, there were none, and our initiative was approved.

Anticipate obstacles

This is another important step Nehemiah took that many leaders overlook. In Nehemiah 2:7-8, we see this: "And I said to the King, 'If it please the King, let letters be given me for the governors of the provinces beyond the river, that they may allow me to pass through until I come to Judah, and a letter to Asaph, the keeper of the King's forest, that he may give me timber to make beams for the gates of the fortress which is by the Temple, for the wall of the city and for the house to which I will go.'" Often, leaders make plans and do not anticipate issues that can arise from their decisions. Thus, they wind up spending enormous amounts of time solving unintended problems they helped create by inadequate planning.

Establish priorities

Any good plan must have clear priorities. We see later in Nehemiah 2 that he went out at night and inspected the wall. What was he doing? He was continuing his thinking and preparation process by considering priorities.

Engage the right people

Nehemiah only took a few men with him to inspect the wall. He said, "I did not tell anyone what God was putting into my mind to do for Jerusalem." He apparently took men who were most trustworthy and could help the most in planning this massive project. Engaging the right people is critical for any leader. When Jethro advised Moses to engage other leaders and share the load with them, he told Moses to find trustworthy leaders (Exodus 18:21). In 1 Kings 12:6, the young and new King Rehoboam consulted two groups of people. He asked the elders who had served his father, Solomon, what to do. They said "If you will be a servant to this people today, and will serve them and grant them their petition, and speak good words to them, then they will be your servant forever." Sadly for him, he did not listen to their counsel. Instead, he went to the young men who grew up with him. They told him to show his leadership by abusive strength and not by service or kindness. Because Rehoboam took the advice of his friends, most people quit following him and rejected him as king. Engaging the right people and listening to them is a key characteristic of any successful leader.

Engage people properly

People's personality profiles help predict what they will contribute to the team effort and in how to properly engage them. The dominant personality, for example, is going to speak quickly, make decisions quickly, and want to take control. Once a project is well planned, it's fine for that person to be the project coordinator. The influencer personalities are going to speak quickly and often and are willing to promote the project and care for the people aspects of the initiative. The steady personalities are going to be responsible for doing much of the work. They know how to do the work and are great team members. They do not speak up as quickly. Therefore, you must create a comfortable forum for their input or ask for it directly and encourage them to share their perspectives. The compliant or cautious personalities are going to think of detailed questions to ask and anticipate problems that nobody else is thinking about. They also are generally going to be hesitant to speak up. But it's critical that their insights be sought and heeded. A great number of mistakes can be avoided by listening to these people. Also, oftentimes they are able to improve upon already good ideas. Leaders without training or perspective on the unique personality profiles of their team are going to have a difficult time engaging people correctly.

Cast the vision

In Nehemiah 2: 17, he said, "You see the bad situation we are in, that Jerusalem is desolate and its gates burned by fire. Come, let us rebuild the wall of Jerusalem so that we will no longer be a reproach." Notice that Nehemiah said that they were in a bad situation. He could have portrayed the people as in a mess and himself as their savior. Yet he did not elevate himself above the people or criticize them for their role in Jerusalem's demise. He opened up and shared his heart with the people. "I told them how the hand of my God had been favorable to me and also about the King's words which he had spoken to me" (Nehemiah 2:18). He encouraged the people that they had God's support and the king's support to undertake this great project.

Share the vision

In verse 18, we see the response of the people as they said, "Let us arise and build." This vision was not something Nehemiah dreamed up on his own. It was what God put in his heart to do. He simply articulated the vision and encouraged the people. But he did it in a way that it inspired them, and it became a shared vision because they said "Let us arise and build." Many leaders ride into town like a new sheriff calling attention to themselves, assigning blame and criticizing others, barking out orders, and expecting compliance. That was not Nehemiah's way at all. He came as a servant. He did not demand any of the rights he had as governor, and he shared the vision with the people in a way that provoked them to own it and become excited about it.

Share the work

Nehemiah led the work, but people did the work. However, people did the work for which they volunteered and which they most wanted to do. Nehemiah was a very astute leader. Nehemiah 3 says most of the people rebuilt the section of the wall in front of their house. This allowed people to do the portion of the work about which they were most passionate, and they did it with great care and enthusiasm.

Application

I. Does your planning process start with prayer?
_____
_____
_____

II. Do you anticipate unintended consequences?
_____
_____
_____

III. Do you engage the right people in the planning process?
_____
_____
_____

IV. Do you engage them in the right way – considering their personality profiles?
_____
_____
_____

V. Is the final vision a shared vision?
_____
_____
_____
_____

Chapter 2

YOU CAN'T MAKE PROGRESS "FIGHTING FIRES"

Thought:
Have you ever wondered how much you could get done if you weren't "putting out fires" all the time?

"Without consultation, plans are frustrated, but with many counselors they succeed."

Proverbs 15:22

Ask people if they like change. Some will say yes, others say no, and others will say it depends. Some personality types tend to like change. Some are more comfortable with the status quo. But we know people want progress. They expect to do better next year than they did this year. How is that possible if the organization doesn't make progress? That leads us to a key principle for making progress.

Avoid "fire fighting"

Making progress in organizations is like making money in your investment portfolio. The first rule is preserve capital. The second rule is preserve capital. And the third rule is don't forget rules number one and two. Stated more plainly, the first rule of making money is don't lose money. Don't go backwards.

Organizational progress is like climbing a mountain. You can only get to the top if you don't stumble and fall to the bottom. It reminds me of professional sports. Sometimes, a team goes on the field and plays a superior game, defeating an able opponent. They won. Yet frequently games are decided by one team committing more errors than the other. In football, excessive penalties can cause the loss of games. Sometimes it's a dropped pass that hits the receiver in the chest and should have been caught. Sometimes it's a missed tackle. The list goes on and on. My point is, I've seen more professional football games lost due to errors than I have seen won due to superior play.

> **Basic errors often cause teams to lose.**

The same thing happens in basketball. I've seen national championship games lost because of a low shooting percentage from the free-throw line. Games sometimes are decided by missed layups, unnecessary fouls, or technical fouls due to flaring tempers.

Chapter 2 – "You Can't Make Progress Fighting Fires"

You may ask, "What does this have to do with organizations?" Everything! I see the same thing in business and other organizations. Our goals seem to be oriented toward hitting a homerun, the grand slam rather than consistently getting singles with no errors. How many times have we seen large, well-established businesses go bankrupt because of substantial errors? Their business models were not flawed. Their employees were good and talented. But someone, usually the leadership, made a mistake that took the company down.

> **Everyone hitting a single is going to win nearly every game. <u>Occasionally</u>, you may win because of a "grand slam."**

The first key to getting ahead is don't go backwards

Avoiding errors, anticipating unintended consequences, and being proactive are the keys to not going backward.

I dealt with a handful of turnaround situations in my career and referred to them as "firefighting" situations.

> **It's hard to get ahead in organizational life when you're fighting fires all the time.**

The organizations spent an inordinate amount of time dealing with problems. Consequently, the people worked extremely hard but couldn't make any progress. The natural tendency of leaders was just to work harder to put out the fires and try to eke out some progress. My approach was to triage the fires.

Empowering Progress

Metaphorically speaking, I first determined if it was a gas fire, wood fire, or brushfire. Gas fires cannot be put out by pouring water on them. Organizationally, these are the types of fires that don't go away with just more time and energy. The source of the problems has to be identified and stopped, as with a literal gas fire. These are systemic problems. One of the most important things a leader can do in a turn-around situation is to identify and stop systemic problems.

Next, I identified the wood burning fires. These fires are very hot and will "burn the house down." They are worth the time and energy to put out in an organization and are a high priority.

The brush fires will burn themselves out without much damage if left alone. There are some problems in an organization that are isolated and will go away if left alone.

When I went into turnaround situations, I first distinguished between the small fires and the big fires. I learned some small fires will burn out, but the big fires will "burn the house down." I also learned some small fires will become big fires and "burn the house down." So I focused on the root-cause issues and took action on those things that were causing big fires. A lot of the problems in organizations are systemic. If you don't get to the root cause, they will happen repeatedly, consuming enormous time. My experience as an internal auditor taught me to look for systemic problems rather than isolated ones.

Fixing the root cause of big problems will free up a lot of time in a "fire-fighting" organization. After root-cause problems are fixed, leaders should put out the smaller fires that have potential to become really big fires—wood burning fires. That saves another big block of time down the road. Understand that in the meantime, some of the smaller fires burned out by themselves—brush fires.

After the fires are extinguished, you can take time previously used for firefighting and spend it on something productive, moving the organization forward. When I went to Physician Services, the first year was spent taking action to prevent big fires and putting out the major fires. It was the second year when we began to make progress.

Chapter 2 – "You Can't Make Progress Fighting Fires"

Many otherwise good leaders significantly underestimate the importance of anticipating negative outcomes and avoiding unintended consequences. For example, the big oil company British Petroleum could have prevented the 2010 Deepwater Horizon oil spill and saved billions of dollars by expending very little effort. The same was true of Exxon with the Valdez spill. It was a completely avoidable problem that caused the organization billions of dollars to solve.

So much focus is put on moving ahead that sometimes little attention is paid to those things that will move us backward. Let's think about some practical areas where we overlook opportunities to anticipate problems

THE MOST COMMON AREAS WHERE LEADERS NEED TO ANTICIPATE PROBLEMS

#1 - Personnel selection

Having the right people in place is critical to the success of an organization. Yet many organizations have poor hiring practices. Many leaders are not well trained in handling the interview process. Often, candidates are not vetted well enough. It's not uncommon for organizations to hire people, have problems with them, and find out the same problems existed with previous employers. It would have cost the organization far less to find that out on the front end and not hire the person than to discover it later.

> *"Furthermore, you shall select out of all the people able men who fear God, men of truth, those who hate dishonest gain; and you shall place these over them as leaders."*
> *Exodus 18:21*

Many organizations do not use personality profiles as tools to understand the strengths and weaknesses of candidates they are considering. Because they won't spend the time or money on these perfectly good tools, they don't hire the best people for the job. Even if the people do not fail, they're not the best match for their jobs. There is still an opportunity cost involved.

Not taking time in the recruiting process to get the best people is a very common way organizations fail to avoid serious problems.

#2 - Communications

The second biggest problem I see repeatedly, especially in larger organizations, is the failure to communicate proactively. It's so easy for this to happen. You're really busy. Your gut tells you that you should call certain individuals and give them a headsup or see what they think before you take action. But you think, "It's my decision to make, and I don't have time." You move forward, and people are upset or a mistake is made. The phone call to inform people or ask a question usually would have taken only 10-25% of the amount of time it takes to solve the problem. You multiply this several times a day, and you see the impact of failure to be good at proactive communications.

#3 - Mismatched goals

Alignment of goals among individuals in the organization and among departments in the organization is key to progress. When the organization has one set of goals and the individuals have different goals, what happens? The individual goals win out in the short short-term and may hurt the organization.

"For he who is not against us is for us."
Mark 9:40

"Choose for yourselves today whom ye will serve..."
Joshua 24:15

Chapter 2 – "You Can't Make Progress Fighting Fires"

That individuals pursue their own goals should not surprise leaders. Following our human nature, we are inherently self-focused. As preachers say, there's an "I" in the middle of sin.

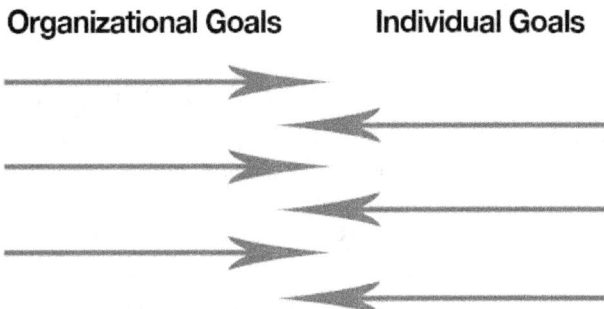

Aligning people with the mission, values, vision, priorities, and accountability measures is key.[2] Anytime this is not done well, individuals are going to pursue their own goals. That's why I recommend reemphasizing the organization's goals on an annual basis. It's also why I recommend verifying throughout the year that the priorities of leaders and employees are aligned.

When individuals don't agree with the goals of the organization, at a minimum they don't pursue them aggressively. At worst, they work consciously or maybe subconsciously against them.

People need to be working toward a common goal for the organization to succeed.

Competition within your own team

Among facilities owned by the same company, there is often competition rather than cooperation. I remember a hospital system that owned several hospitals in a major market. One of the hospitals had 90% of the obstetrics (OB) market share. Another hospital nearby decided this was a good, profitable business. They decided to convert existing space and started an OB program. After some time, the first hospital had 50% of the market share. The second hospital had 40% market share. The problem was both facilities were owned by the same organization. It had the same 90% market share as before but had overhead in two facilities competing for the same patients. In large organizations with multiple units, it takes good planning to align objectives so entities cooperate rather than compete.

When I led Physician Services at HCA, we created regional recruiting offices. One benefit of the regional offices was the ability to maximize our opportunity to sign a physician into our system while minimizing the expense. Information was gathered regarding physicians' geographic preferences, and they were sometimes flown for interviews to an area with five company-owned hospitals. With one trip, the company was able to let the physician evaluate multiple openings and align them with the one that best suited them. This increased the chance of being able to recruit the physician to an HCA hospital, and it minimized expenses by accomplishing multiple interviews in one trip.

Before this system was created, three hospitals with physician needs might use different recruiting firms to meet their recruiting needs. Therefore, a physician was flown in by the recruiting firm to visit one hospital. Sometimes the recruiting firms also recruited for the competition. That meant there could be times when the physician visited an HCA hospital and that of a competitor with HCA paying the expenses. The new model eliminated that. So you would think everyone would have been delighted.

Yet there was a fair amount of conflict over this model. Hospital A didn't care about the needs of hospital B. They didn't care that hospital B might be the best fit for that physician, upping the chances of signing and keeping him for the long term. They were interested in signing the physician at their facility. You see, the goals were not sufficiently aligned within a market to encourage cooperation among hospitals rather than competition. In large organizations, there is competition among departments, operating units, and individuals all the time. It takes great diligence in the planning process to minimize it.

Chapter 2 – "You Can't Make Progress Fighting Fires"

Conflicting goals

I remember a time when the company went through a major computer conversion. The information technology teams were incentivized based on the number of conversions accomplished during the year. I was in internal audit at the time and raised questions about the quality of conversions. I believed if conversions were not handled well, it would impact the revenue cycle and increase bad debts. The company had just been through a major merger, and the individuals who decided to incentivize conversions based on volume alone had never seen computer conversions on that scale. I wasn't able to get my message across.

After six months, the revenue cycle had been so impacted and bad debts had increased so much in converted facilities, that it was impacting results for the entire company. The conversions were halted until the quality dimensions could be addressed.

It is common in large organizations for departments and operating units to have ill-conceived goals that hurt the operating units and the entire company. It often takes better planning than exists in even sophisticated organizations to ensure well thought out alignment of goals.

I have a friend who buys distressed companies, turns them around, and eventually sells them. Frequently, these are subsidiaries within larger companies. Many times these subsidiaries are not doing well because they do not receive the appropriate focus and attention. Their goals are not sufficiently aligned with those of the parent organization to make meaningful contributions. Therefore, it is better for the organizations to spin them out than to keep them.

Employees can have a great deal of fun and achieve fulfillment in organizations where goals are clear, consistent with their talents and passions, and well aligned. This blesses the employees and brings productivity to the organizations. Without goal alignment, employees are stressed, confused, unproductive, and uncommitted. If you want to bless employees and have a productive organization, make sure goals are aligned.

REALIGN GOALS WITH ACCOUNTABILITY SYSTEMS WHEN CHANGE OCCURS

It is easy, especially in large organizations, to set up financial incentive systems and be too slow to change them as the environment changes. In the health care system, for instance, the ability to measure the quality of the care and incentivize hospitals to improve care began changing. In a particular system, the CEO kept focusing on quality results. Professionals were hired to help improve quality of care. But things seemed to change very little. The year this organization changed its financial incentives for all its leaders to include reward for improvement in the quality scores at hospitals, there was a marked improvement.

This is a great reminder to leaders. When the environment changes, you have to change the accountability structure for your team in order to get a different result. Simply talking about it, saying you want to see something different, criticizing people for not changing, and even threatening to do something if there's no change doesn't do anything. When you change the accountability system to line up with the goals, behavior starts to change quickly.

LISTENING – THE KEY TO AVOIDING A "FIREFIGHTING" CULTURE

It's obvious that not going backward is crucial in organizational life. So how do we make sure we don't go backward? Listening to other people is key in this process.

> *"Without consultation, plans are frustrated, but with many counselors, they succeed."*
> *Proverbs 15:22*

Different personality profiles see different slices of the world. Some tend to see the opportunities. Some tend to see the impact on people. Others tend to be implementers and see the practical steps to make something

Chapter 2 – "You Can't Make Progress Fighting Fires"

work. They will also see when something will not work. Some personalities will tend to see pitfalls and find ways to improve upon an idea. When you get all these perspectives involved in solving a problem or creating a plan, you have much greater chances of moving forward without creating more problems to be solved down the road. One challenge in organizations is that the aggressive, risk-taking personalities don't like to seek and listen to the advice of the more process-oriented personalities that could help them avoid pitfalls. This is exacerbated by the fact that the people who understand the process best and are most capable of improving it tend not to speak up until asked. The aggressive types often dismiss the wise counsel of these individuals should they volunteer advice.

The CEO who listened

I'm thinking of different CEOs I've seen in operation. One had the best vision and was perhaps the most gifted intellectually that I had ever encountered. I can think of numerous times when people offered dissenting views, but he was right. Yet there were a couple of areas where people tried to give him counsel, and he refused to listen.

> *"Before destruction the heart of man is haughty,*
> *but humility goes before honor."*
> *Proverbs 18:12*

They were pretty fundamental areas, but he continued down the same path. He eventually lost his job as CEO. This man was among the hardest working CEOs I had ever met. He was also one of the smartest people I've ever met. Yet he lost his job primarily because he reached a point where he no longer valued other people's perspectives.

I contrast this CEO with another CEO. He was also exceptionally talented. Yet for important decisions, he consulted more people than anyone I've encountered. And when he wasn't solving problems, he still asked people he met in the organization for their perspectives. From the executive suite to the boiler room in the basement, he asked for people's opinions and really listened to them. His knowledge was so strengthened by multiple perspectives that there was never a big mistake made on his watch.

Individual application

Anticipating problems is critical in leaders' personal lives as well as their organizations. In fact, many organizational problems result from poor personal choices. What are some individual problems that shipwreck careers and affect organizations? Just like King David's affair affected the kingdom of Israel, affairs in organizational life cause leaders to fail and affect their organizations negatively.

Another problem is excessive drinking or drugs. A number of careers of up-and-coming executives have been derailed by getting drunk at the wrong function or by becoming addicted and crashing in their personal lives.

Yet another problem is being a workaholic. Family is ignored, resulting in divorce, which impacts the person's whole life, including the organization. Often, in smaller privately owned organizations, a divorce can ruin the business.

Application

I. What are the three potential problems that could cause your organization to fail?

1._____

2._____

3._____

II. What do you struggle with personally that could cause you to fail?

1._____

2._____

3._____

III. Do you do a good job:

- Selecting people?
- Communicating proactively?

What do you need to change?

_____
_____
_____
_____

IV. Are there departments or teams in your organization that tend to compete or fight with each other rather than cooperate with each other?

Are their goals and incentives aligned? Yes____ No____

If not, what will you change?

_____
_____
_____
_____

V. Do you get the perspectives of others before making major decisions?

Yes____ No____

If not, what will you do in the future?

_____
_____
_____
_____

Chapter 3

LEADING CHANGE

> **Thought:**
> What potential are you giving up by not being proactive in leading change?

*"... but one thing I do:
forgetting what lies behind
and reaching forward to what lies ahead."*

Philippians 3:13

Dick Wells, author of *Sixteen Stones*, says the difference between your present position and your vision is the change necessary to achieve your desired future.[3] Though all organizations experience change, the initial reaction to change generally is either skepticism or outright resistance, in my experience, unless people are already clamoring for change. Some leaders avoid making changes until they have to because of the tendency of some people not to like change.

Auditors tend to be particularly comfortable with the status quo. I would get some resistance every year when we did our plans and plotted changes. I would ask, "Do you want a year with no change?" Most employees in the internal audit department said yes. I said "Are you sure?" And they said, "Yes." I said, "Let me remind you, no change means no compensation increases or promotions." They quickly said, "No, we want those changes."

I applied the idea to the broader company, showing that if we didn't change anything to grow profits, there would not be money for merit or promotional increases. When the team understood that change was necessary for progress, they were open to change.

How Not to Lead Change

First, let me tell you what doesn't work. Early in my career, I had just assumed leadership responsibilities for the internal audit department at HCA. The culture, the processes, and the results all needed to change. The department needed to gain more credibility, and it needed to happen within a year. I locked myself away in my office for a few days, including some weekend time. I came up with goals that I saw as critical to what we needed to accomplish in the next year.

I called a meeting of my direct reports and proudly laid out the goals and initiatives that we would need to accomplish. I waited for my team to respond, expecting them to be impressed with the thoroughness of my work, the soundness of the plans, and have a great deal of appreciation for the fact that I figured all this out for the team without requiring their input. It seems so foolish now, but I was genuinely surprised at their near rebellion. It wasn't that they didn't think the plans were good; they were simply overwhelmed by them. Being a new leader, I did the only thing I could think of. I retreated!

I asked them what they thought were the most important changes we needed to make. They told me. I asked them what we could get done in the next month. We wrote down their answers and all agreed. I asked which of those changes we could make in the next week. We wrote those down and agreed. We did this every week for a month and, at the end of the month, had accomplished more than we thought we could do that first month. We went through the process for another month. We made plans weekly and monitored progress. At the end of the second month, we had accomplished more than we had targeted for the month.

Now I could see the team was getting momentum. So we tried the same process, but this time we set goals for the next three months and monitored progress monthly. At the end of three months, we had exceeded the goals we set. We continued to do this for the balance of the year. At the end of the year, we had accomplished more than the goals and initiatives I had outlined initially.

Leader's role in the change process

A critical role of leadership in an organization is to lead the change efforts. It can be frustrating because it's not easy. It tends to cause tension, and many times the improvement sought is not achieved. So, why is there so much tension and resistance if change is necessary for progress and people tend to want progress?

Change is uncomfortable and inefficient

Leaders must guide their organizations through change even though it isn't comfortable for many people. It's especially uncomfortable for certain personality types that do a lot of the work in organizations. Plus, change is inefficient initially. It is like taking one step backward and two steps forward. Actually, that would be the picture of a successful change. An unsuccessful change would be two steps backward and one step forward. A neutral change would be one step backward and one step forward.

> **1 step back and 2 forward = Good change**
> **1 step back and 1 forward = Neutral change**
> **2 steps back and 1 forward = Bad change**

Leaders often have ideas for improvement. It's very clear to them that a certain change will be an improvement over the old way of doing things. They get excited about the impact of their new idea. It's such a good idea that they forget some people tend not to like change. Then, when people don't wholeheartedly embrace the change, they get upset.

Leaders need to remember that even good changes can necessitate substantial periods of adaptation. Think about the children of Israel in the Bible. Moses led them out of slavery, and they were free. But almost immediately they began to complain. There were aspects of their enslaved lives that they remembered and missed. Even though the change was positive, living through it seemed hard.

This principle is particularly evident surrounding computer conversions. People will beg and almost cry for better technology. Then new software is implemented. Now the screens and reports don't look the same. Even though they may be better, it takes longer to do what the employees used to do. It's not long before people are literally crying and wishing they had the old system back.

Blind to the need

Often, leaders don't see the need for change. I remember as an auditor asking questions about how things were done at various facilities. One of the most common responses was, "Well, we've always done it that way." Consultants hear that a lot. "We've always done it that way and its worked fine so far, so why should we change it?"

The reason it should be changed often is because it can be done a lot better, but that can be hard to see. When we create processes and refine them over time, we tend to think we've made them as good as they can be. It takes a fresh look to see things from a different perspective. I learned this when I got opportunities to lead new departments at HCA. I looked and asked questions and saw potential changes that could lead to improvement. They were obvious to me. I did not create any of the processes. I had not hired any of the people. So I could see things objectively and spot needed changes.

My ability to see opportunities for improvement only lasted one or two years though. After that period of time, I had created and refined enough processes and formed an affinity to the team. So it became difficult for me to see what needed to change. I had to get the perspectives of other people through paid consultants or individuals in the company further removed from what I was doing.

I use the analogy of people standing next to their house with their noses pressed against the window. When you're in that position, you can't tell what the front of the house looks like or see if there are bricks falling off the house. Yet perfect strangers who know nothing about your house and have never seen it before can stand in the driveway and have a broader view. They can spot obvious things that you're unable to see from your perspective. Sometimes organizations need consultants for their specialized expertise. But often consultants simply come in with an objective perspective and gather information the leader did not have time to gather, summarize it, and give It to the leadership.

I could see things much more objectively when I was given the opportunity to lead new divisions. I did not know the history of the people. I had not implemented processes, policies, or procedures. I was able look at everything without any emotional attachment. But after a year or two, I would lose my objectivity.

There is a great benefit to making small strategic changes over time. There is less risk of failure in making the change. But sometimes the biggest risk is in not making a big change. Sometimes, big opportunities come along or the big problem shows up and small changes are not enough. Sometimes, we are faced with making a major change for a strategic opportunity that will not present itself again or solving a problem that has the potential to severly damage the organization.

Fear of failure

Often, leaders hesitate to make strategic changes they believe will benefit their organizations because there is a risk of immediate failure and criticism. Therefore, they defer change until they feel they have no choice. I have personally hesitated to make tough personnel changes and others changes I knew needed to be made because there was risk of criticism if I was wrong or didn't execute the changes well. We shouldn't underestimate the fear and doubt leaders often experience in making changes of substance. It didn't get easier with time or experience for me. The more success we have, the more it seems we are unwilling to risk our reputations on making important but risky changes when there are other options.

THE KEYS TO LEADING CHANGE

Involve the team

One of the first keys is to let people have a say in change that affects them. They're much more accepting of change they help plan. Nehemiah was masterful at this. When they have input and involvement in making the plans and setting the deadlines, people feel ownership and commitment that doesn't exist when plans are simply announced. Plus, you usually avoid unintended consequences, or you get better ideas by having them involved. Remember, the "S" and "C" temperaments are going to see unintended consequences that the "D" and "I" temperaments don't.

We can take a cue from Jesus. He wants to change our lives and change them radically. Yet in Revelation 3:20 we read, "Behold I stand at the door and knock. If any man will open it, I will come in…." Think about this. If the creator of our universe waits for an invitation to come in and change us, shouldn't we think long and hard about forcing people to change? It's much better to invite and lead change than to force it.

Set goals the team believes are achievable

The next key is to set goals everyone thinks are achievable. In my case, the team was overwhelmed with the goals I laid out for the year. By contrast, Nehemiah only asked the people to build the wall six inches per day.[3] Time proved my plans were achievable because we achieved even more. But it was more than the team could absorb at the time. People's experiences and personality profiles determine the timeframes in which changes need to be accomplished. Some personalities can get overwhelmed. Others tend to set goals too high. Some leaders, knowing people tend to fight change, assume they should force it and get it over with. That does work sometimes, but you always pay a price for it and it's risky. Sometimes a forced change at work is the "straw that breaks the camel's back" for employees. When team members respond differently than usual to a pressure or perceived threat, it's wise to quickly sit with them and try to understand what else is going on in their lives. Most of the time, I find their behavior or attitude is driven by something other than work circumstances. By understanding that, we can avoid damaging relationships and causing problems downstream in our organizations.

Share the credit

In Nehemiah 8, after the wall-building project was completed, Nehamiah called a great gathering of the people. Unlike many leaders who would call such a gathering and take most of the credit for success, Nehemiah brought no attention to himself. Rather, he put priests in charge of the event. They celebrated their success. Nehemiah acknowledged the work of every group of people. He didn't brag only about the top performers. He acknowledged the amount of work they did, but he didn't criticize the ones who did the least. Rather, he acknowledged what they did to contribute to the success fo the whole project. Nehemiah didn't take any of the credit. He didn't seek the approval or accolades of the people. Nehemiah only asked for one thing: he asked God to remember his service and sacrifice.

THE MUSTARD SEED AND LEAVEN (YEAST) APPROACH TO CHANGE

God's approach to making change is quite simple and can be illustrated from Matthew 13. Though this passage is about the Kingdom of God and not change in organizations, it highlights principles that can be applied to change. From the parable of the mustard seed in Matthew 13:31, we see the importance of starting small and letting something grow over time. From the parable of the leaven in Matthew 13:34, we see the importance of growth or change at a steady, measured pace. Remember Nehemiah again. He only asked the people to build six inches of wall per day.

Chapter 3 – Leading Change

WHY DON'T LEADERS START SMALL AND GROW AT A MEASURED PACE?

It seems like such a simple principle. So why don't people do it? Well, there are several reasons:

I. Pride

Politicians could make dramatic changes over five, ten, and fifteen year periods if they used a biblical approach to change. So why don't they? Often the answer seems to be pride. Politicians want to be known for some spectacular bill and go down in history. Working with a team to accomplish smaller results over a longer period of time without fanfare is not attractive to them.

> *"Before destruction, the heart of man is haughty, but humility goes before honor."*
> *Proverbs 18:12*

Even as I write this book, our nation is in a terrible mess. The politicians hold to their extreme positions to please voters and, therefore, take no action. There are many things both political parties could agree upon that would be good for the nation and could be enacted immediately. Yet they refuse to compromise and take a measured approach.

There is an old saying, "It's amazing what you can get accomplished when you don't care who gets the credit." We can see the truth of this in politics for certain. And it's true in business too. Corporate departments work against each other based on pride and ego rather than for the good of the whole organization because they want to control what happens and be able to take credit.

Churches, ministries, and nonprofit organizations aren't exempt from this either. Seldom do they try to make small changes. Instead, they create big initiatives and programs. Often the motives are pure, but not always. Sometimes the leaders are seeking recognition.

II. Fear

A successful executive coach told me the greatest barrier to success he saw in the life of executives was having the courage to act. They knew what they should do but were afraid to do it. This really struck a chord with me. I can think of numerous times I knew what to do but didn't act or delayed taking action because of fear. I see the same phenomenon in others. They know what's right but want to play it politically safe rather than speak up and take the lead in an initiative that won't be popular. Pride and fear are actually two sides of the same coin. Our pride causes us not to take risk because we fear failure and loss of reputation and status in our organizations.

III. Procrastination

Leaders have a lot going on every day. Often they find themselves just trying to keep up. The thought of resistance and potentially failing with change makes procrastination very easy. Because changes are not planned and implemented systematically through the year, leaders find themselves responding to crisis situations in which big changes have to be tried quickly.

IV. Lack of planning/clear priorities

Implementing change by starting small and growing at a measured pace requires clear priorities and constant planning. Leaders who aren't committed to progressive change will get distracted and find themselves in crisis situations implementing major changes quickly.

V. Hurry

Some leaders are just in a hurry. They are anxious and impatient. When they decide they want something done, they want it done right then. They tend to like big initiatives. So they don't slow down and plan incremental changes. They force change through their organizations and make people feel they're drinking out of a fire hydrant. They are impatient and can't see the potential problems associated with hurried change.

BENEFITS OF STARTING SMALL AND GROWING SLOWLY

Starting small allows us to do pilot testing and float "trial balloons" before making a larger commitment. With this approach, we also tend to get less pushback from people comfortable with the status quo. We observe businesses doing this all the time. HCA piloted new computer software before large scale rollouts. Restaurants pilot new menus in key markets before making nationwide changes.

Starting small

If I had a 300-page book and asked people to read it, many would feel overwhelmed. They would begin to explain how busy they were and how it would be near impossible for them to read the book with everything else going on. If I gave them the same book and asked if they could take ten minutes to read ten pages that day, most people would say yes. If I did that for thirty days, they would have read the 300-page book. I have actually used this approach to get feedback on this book as I have written it. I have asked people to read a section at a time and give feedback rather than read the whole book at one time.

Often the reason for procrastination is that people feel overwhelmed at the size of a project. That's why it is so important to take big projects and break them in small pieces.

The TV industry has used a gradual approach to impact our culture and society, though not in a positive way. When I had children and started watching reruns of programs from from my childhood, I was struck at the change in language, violence, sexual innuendos, and overall values over thirty years. If the programming we watch today had been aired thirty years ago, there would have been a rebellion and families would have turned off their TVs. But because the change in programming was made gradually, people never rebelled and quit watching.

Pilot testing

This principle applies to computer conversions. After computer software is changed, it is implemented in a pilot program. It stays in the pilot until all the bugs are worked out. It saves considerable time and cost to pilot new software instead of implementing it on a broad scale. Imagine the time and costs required to fix computer bugs at multiple locations. At HCA, for example, we piloted a major computer conversion in one facility rather than implementing it initially at all 300 hospitals the company owned. Imagine the time, cost, disruption to operations, and resistance to change if we had implemented the new software in three hundred facilities rather than one. Pilot projects are designed not to be overwhelming.

Starting small, or "pilot testing," increases efficiency over the long run because problems are avoided. When national restaurant chains want to change their menus, they take a restaurant or a market and pilot the change. They see the reaction to the change. They make any needed modifications and re-test. Then they begin to roll out the change at all their restaurants. If the change is not successful, they haven't failed in three thousand restaurants. They've failed in one restaurant or in one market. Any changes needed are made in the pilot and not three thousand restaurants.

Example

In leading Physician Services, we used the principles of the mustard seed and yeast to expand our initiatives significantly over several years. One example concerned recruiting physicians. In one market we consolidated recruiting efforts with good success. We built on that success and went to other markets in that division. The division began having better success than other divisions in its group. Then consolidated recruiting expanded to another division within the group with good results. After some time, we had implemented the change in all divisions of that group.

Then we went to another group and showed them the results. There was one division within that group that wanted to pilot the program. We implemented it with good results, and other divisions followed until we were running the program in all divisions of that group.

Over three to four years, we implemented the program across the entire company. If we had tried to implement it as one big initiative, it likely would not have succeeded.

We followed a similar process with a hospital-based anesthesia initiative. I believed we were paying too much in anesthesia subsidies because we did not have enough expertise at the local level in many situations. We found an individual who was very qualified to help us, but I couldn't get the approval to put that individual on the payroll. I talked to one division president who was always easy to work with and asked if he would do a pilot where we contracted with this person to handle anesthesia contracting and negotiation as a consultant. I said Physician Services would pay half the cost if his division would pay half. We had enough room in the budget for the consulting fee but couldn't get approval for an added person on the payroll.

We ran the pilot for six months and saved so much money in anesthesia subsidies that we were able to get approval to hire the person fulltime. We did a lot of work and that division showed substantial results. Then we went to other divisions within that group with great results. Over three years, we developed an extensive team and did work throughout the company with many millions of dollars in savings. Without a creative, low-risk approach, this initiative would not have gained traction.

Over twelve years, we added a number of service lines and launched major initiatives within Physician Services. They all had national influence, but every one was started as a pilot and implemented throughout the company gradually. There was not a single one we could have sold as a national initiative from the beginning.

Another important aspect of our successful changes was giving other people the credit at every opportunity. After a successful pilot, we would point to operations and give them the credit.

> *"Do not claim honor in the presence of the King, and do not stand in the place of great men."*
> *Proverbs 25:6*

Our role in the process was always ultimately revealed, and we were given the opportunity to help another division. Small pilots became very large initiatives over time using this approach.

Application in your personal life

Years ago I began running for my health and weight control. About a mile into the run, there was a long uphill grade. I would grit my teeth and try to make it all the way. I would tense up and try harder the further I ran but could never make it. Then I set lower goals. My goal was to get to the next mailbox. Each time I got tired, I looked no further than the next mailbox and asked myself if I could just run that much further. Each time I could. The very first time I used this approach, I made it to the top and kept running.

Over the years, I have found the hardest part of exercising is putting on my shoes. In other words, once I make a commitment to do something, put my shoes on, and get moving, it is easier and I do more than I thought I would. I used to think I had to run or walk a certain number of miles. Just thinking about it some days was overwhelming. So I quit thinking about it. I put on my shoes and decided to walk one mile, which seemed easy. Yet there was never a time I only walked one mile. By the time I walked a mile, I felt better and wanted to walk a second mile. Often, I would do a third or fourth mile. Getting started is part of the battle, and that's easier to do when you set lower goals.

What's the Challenge with Small Measured Changes?

It's a great way to lower risk and gain acceptance from the team, but it's not always possible. Sometimes there is a crisis or a big, time-sensitive opportunity, and you have to act quickly. Certain changes don't lend themselves to the slower approach. Corporate mergers and acquisitions are an example. Because rapid, drastic changes are necessary at times, it's even more important to be diligent about leading smaller change programs when possible.

Still, the world changes quickly. Often competitive landscapes in the business world change very quickly. Sometimes making small changes just isn't the right answer. Operating managers like to be efficient, and small, gradual change is the most efficient form of change. But efficiency isn't the only consideration in business. Around the year 1900, the most efficient buggy whip maker was the last to go out of business. The effective businesses changed their models and were making leather for car seats. Sometimes radical change entails starting something brand new or totally remaking something is required to face the future. Again, I think of the executive coach who said the biggest barrier to success he had seen over the years in leaders was the courage to act, to make change.

Leaders are sometimes hesitant to make radical changes because of the risk of failure and the resistance they feel they'll face. Yet by not making significant changes warrented by the situation, they guarantee their longer-term failure. Sometimes the biggest longterm risks we take are in not taking the necessary short-term risks.

WARNING – IDEA OF THE WEEK LEADERS

Some leaders see themselves as change agents when, in fact, they are simply "idea of the week" leaders. Most organizations of any size have one somewhere. They go by different names, but this is a common one. Change for the sake of change without a clear plan and use of "pilots" to monitor success is not the way to implement change.

Some leaders say the process or people are not working out, and they begin making changes without the counsel of others and without a plan. This often results in no improvement or in the situation getting worse. Too much change, change not well planned, or change that does not involve the team usually yields poor results.

Entrepreneurial leaders in for-profit and nonprofit organizations tend to do this. They are often creative in nature, get bored easily, and make change for the sake of change. There are certain personality profiles that are highly creative and have problems with the status quo. Sometimes they make unnecessary changes. There is a difference between leading continual change toward a vision and "idea of the week" or "idea of the month" leadership.

Application

I. Are you proactively leading changes for your organization? What are the three most important changes you are implementing this year?

1. _____
_____

2. _____
_____

3. _____
_____

II. Are you going to pilot your changes? Yes____ No____

Can you accept the risk if it fails and you didn't pilot it?

III. When change is necessary, do you genuinely seek input from your team, especially the team members with more analytical and probing temperaments? Yes____ No____

IV. What important changes are you putting off?

1. _____
_____

2. _____

3. _____

V. What changes do you need make in your personal life?

1. _____

2. _____

3. _____

Chapter 4

PROGRESS THROUGH DOCUMENTATION AND TRAINING

> **Thought:**
> Have you considered how much time you could save if what you knew was well documented and people were trained?

"Now these things happened as examples for us, so that we would not crave evil things as they also craved."

1 Corinthians 10:6

Dr. Frist, Sr. used to say mankind started making its most significant progress after we learned to write. There was a significant change among mankind after the invention of the printing press. Being able to document what we have learned so each generation doesn't have to "reinvent the wheel" has been significant to our progress. One reason God had men write the Bible was so we could learn from the lives and mistakes of others and wouldn't have to learn everything based on our own experience. This is what 1 Corinthians 10:6 (above) is talking about.

The same principle applies in organizations. When I led the internal audit department, we struggled with turnover. Even though our turnover rate improved, it was still high compared to other departments. That was the nature of the internal audit department because it was used as a training ground and promotional opportunity for many professionals. As we tried to add value to the company through our work, I began to hire specialists in certain areas. They would do great work and take our capabilities to new levels.

They would normally stay about two years before someone else in the company hired them because of their specialized knowledge. Then it felt like we would start all over again with someone new.

So I made a commitment to heavily document everything our specialists knew. We created detailed audit programs. We added supplements to the audit programs explaining in detail the thought process and best methods for completing each step. We designed preprinted work papers to facilitate the consistent gathering of information. Once we did this, we did not lose all the expertise of the person that moved somewhere else in the company. In fact, the replacement was able to get up to speed very quickly and usually improved on what we had already developed.

Following this protocol helped us avoid peaks and valleys in the quality of our work. Over time our expertise grew, and we performed at higher levels. As our department grew, we added staff and individuals trained to perform multiple duties, which was also important for the retention of knowledge. Without good documentation and training, organizations cannot maintain a consistent standard of performance or grow their expertise.

This is one reason small organizations tend to stay small. Everything is known by a few people, and the organization can't grow beyond what they personally know and oversee. Documentation allows an organization to develop and learn from best practices, continue to improve, and efficiently train and engage others in the process so the organization can grow. Such practices help make franchise models so successful.

When documentation and training are done properly, new hires don't start from scratch. They begin with the documented knowledge of the previous job holders and often are able to add their unique perspectives and experience to improve the results. It's much quicker and more efficient to bring people up to speed with good documents.

Developing the human capital of the organization should be one goal of any leader, especially in service organizations. If you want a comprehensive management-development course for your team, I recommend you consider Model-Netics from Main Event Management. This course can be taught to people at every level of the organization. Its use of models makes the material memorable and easier to use among a team that has had the training. Operating managers teach the course to their people so that it applies to their circumstances.

Application

I. Do you have good documentation of your:

    A. Mission?

    B. Values?

    C. Vision?

    D. Organizational objectives?

    E. Organization chart?

    F. Policies and procedures?

    G. Control systems?

    H. Exception reporting systems?

    I. Information systems?

II. In which areas do you need to improve your documentation and training?

_____
_____
_____
_____
_____
_____

Chapter 5

PROGRESS THROUGH ENABLING CONTROL SYSTEMS

> **Thought:**
> How much more could you relax if you had an easy way of knowing things in your organization were in control? If you had a system to keep things on track, how much time and energy would you save?

"So then each one of us will give an account of himself to God."

Romans 14:12

One great challenge many entrepreneurs face is empowering others and letting go appropriately. They do not know how to empower. Consequently, they keep control. The behavior I see ranges from ultimate micromanagement, with leaders' "thumbs in every pie," to giving instructions without ever following up on the end result.

God's approach to control

If we are going to be godly leaders, we should look at how God handles this issue of control. In this area, I see two erroneous views of God. There are those who believe God is an over-controlling micromanager who does everything He can to make sure we do not enjoy life, punishes us every time we get off track, and wants to keep us from fulfilling our legitimate desires. Then there are those who believe God is uninterested and uninvolved and that everything in life happens according to chance.

In reality, God empowers but also controls appropriately. After the universe was created, Scripture says God gave man dominion over the garden and every living creature (Genesis 1:28). That seems like a God who empowers. He lets go. He gives people freedom with His creation.

So what about control? In the beginning, God only had one rule: not to eat from the tree of the knowledge of good and evil (Genesis 2:17). God gave Adam and Eve permission to eat from any tree or plant in the garden with the exception of that one single tree. That doesn't seem like micromanagement to me. There was only one rule. And what was the purpose of the rule? Was the purpose to restrict their freedom? Was the purpose to restrict their enjoyment of paradise? No! The purpose was to protect them from what God knew would harm them. But they ate the fruit of the tree. It changed their way of life and excluded them from life inside a beautiful garden.

Later, amid the fallen world, God gave humans more rules, which we know as the Ten Commandments. One purpose of the Ten Commandments was human flourishing. All ten were designed to protect and preserve mankind's relationship with God and to enhance their relationship with others. God gave people these commands to protect them. They were to create more enjoyment and fulfillment in life, not less.

Chapter 5 – Progress Through Enabling Control Systems

As time went on, God's people rebelled more, and God continued to give them direction through rules—always intended to guide and protect them. The rules were never mere expressions of control or capricious exertions of God's power, showing His strength or limiting the people's freedom and enjoyment of life. They were always to guide and protect—to keep people from hurting themselves or one another and to maximize their enjoyment of life. Jesus said, "I came that you might have life and have it more abundantly." Some translations say "have it to the full" (John 10:10).

Have you noticed yet that every time people were not lined up with God's mission and followed their own plans, He had to implement more rules to protect them against themselves? In our organizations, the less people are aligned with the mission, vision, and values, the more rules we have to make. It is far better to have greater alignment so we can have fewer rules.

The lesson of the river

We learn a lot about God through nature. A river reminds me of how He works. I sometimes ask people what a river has that other bodies of water do not. They quickly come to the conclusion that river has a current that gives it movement. Then they point out the river has banks to guide it.

A river is constituted by millions of drops of water that fall during a rain, run into streams, then run into creeks, and finally join the river. The water is in motion. The banks of the river do not micromanage each drop of water but rather gently guide the river.

Now think of how a good organization functions. People, tasks, and activities are not micromanaged. Rather, they are guided gently by boundaries that direct them toward the organization's vision. What in an organization creates the current or movement? The organization's vision and priorities, as well as its goals for each individual, create the movement.

What creates the boundaries equivalent to the banks of river? There are several things that create boundaries: policies and procedures, operating manuals, standards for performance, training, accountability systems, and so on.

Why should these be created? To enable individuals to accomplish the mission and vision of the organization. Some people and certain personality types like control just for the sake of exercising control. After many years of being an auditor, I have a firm belief that control systems should never be about control just for the sake of control. Nor should they limit an individual's freedom unless they also protect people and are in the best interests of the organization.

Swamp analogy

If you took away the banks of a river, what would you have over time? It would become a swamp, wouldn't it? What is a swamp like? First of all, it stinks because the water has become stagnant. Next, it's very easy to get lost in a swamp because there is no flow of water or banks to give direction. Third, swamps are dangerous for human beings. There are a lot of surprises in swamps and almost none of them are positive.

Now, let's think about what an organizational swamp would look like. I've seen a number of them in my organizational career. First, the culture stinks because everything is stagnant. Next, there is no flow or direction because vision of the organization is not clear. And, finally, people are just trying to survive. They're lost and don't know how to get out but don't feel safe staying in.

So how do you turn organizational swamps into rivers that have life, direction, and flow? Here is what I did. As a foundation, we clarified why the organization existed—mission. Then, we discovered God's vision for what the organization should become. Next, we created strategies and tactics to accomplish the vision. Finally, those were broken into goals for individuals with an accountability system for achieving them. This created energy and current for the organization. Then appropriate policies and procedures, operating manuals, training systems, and enabling control systems were put into place to guide people and activities.

Organizational flooding

We just saw what happens if the river banks get too wide—an organizational swamp is created. Now let's look at what happens if the banks get too narrow. If you had a big river that was a mile wide and suddenly narrowed the banks down to one half mile, what would happen? That's right, flooding! Where there is too much water and the banks are too narrow, water moves outside the banks and creates damage in surrounding areas.

How does flooding in organizations occur? Usually, large amounts of change are enacted that cannot be accommodated by the existing boundaries of the organization. When the boundaries are too narrow to accommodate new goals and assignments, people, trying to achieve their goals, work around the existing boundaries, seeing them as barriers. Now instead of having control, the organization has lost total control. I've seen this happen many times and it's dangerous to the organization.

This issue of setting boundaries and vision for an organization is very important. Remember Scripture says where there is no vision, the people perish. In organizational life, if there is not a clear vision and the boundaries are too broad, it becomes an organizational swamp. By contrast, if boundaries are not broad enough to accommodate the vision, you have organizational flooding where people work around existing boundaries and all control is lost.

Empowering while having control

In Lee Iacocca's book, he describes his turnaround efforts at Chrysler. One thing he did was quarterly reviews or accountability sessions with each of his vice presidents. This is a practice I adapted and with good results. If this method is used properly, it's not possible for your direct reports to be off track relative to their annual goals for more than ninety days without your knowing it. Of course, I had more frequent contact and follow-up, but these quarterly reviews were comprehensive in nature. At the end of the year, my direct reports had already had the three reviews with me regarding their progress. Therefore, the annual review was easy to accomplish, and there were no surprises.

Finally, let's talk about how you set boundaries. If possible, all four personality profiles from the standard DISC personality profile should be involved in this process. The "D" profile likes to feel in control but doesn't like getting into details and will tend to delegate the establishment of policies and procedures, operating manuals, and controls. The "I" personality doesn't like getting into the details and tends to feel controls are abusive.

The "S" personality is good at developing operating manuals, knowing how things are done, and appropriately establishing manuals, policies procedures, and controls. The "C" personality will tend to be more detail oriented and risk-averse, and will design very tight controls. In many larger organizations, the "C" personality will volunteer to create the boundaries. When you don't have all four personality profiles involved, you will tend to get boundaries too narrow and the flow of the organization will be restricted. Then people simply comply and are not creative and proactive, or they rebel, work around the system, and you have less control.

On the other hand, good and well-balanced control systems help detect problems early before they get too big, and they help keep us on track toward meaningful progress. What does a control system look like? From my experience, the simpler, the better. HCA had operating indicator reports that showed the standard performance level for a given position, an individual's actual performance, and the variance. Varying degrees of follow-up were initiated based on the degree of variance and its impact.

Why expectations are not met

Some expectations are easy to express in measurable standards, and some are a bit harder. The most common reasons expectations are not met are:

- The expectations are not clear or the employee did not understand them or how they would be measured.

- There are too many expectations and some do not get appropriate focus.

- An expectation gap is not addressed in a timely manner by the leader.

Following up on unmet expectations in a reasonable timeframe is key in clarifying standards. Any gap in understanding can be resolved so that you do not go for an extended period of time with an important expectation not being met. One of the biggest reasons leaders do not get the expected results is that they do not follow up to ensure an expectation gap is narrowed or some plan of action is created.

Church example

Though it's been over ten years, my kids still delight in telling about the time they claim I kicked the ministers at church out of a management development class. My recollection of the story is different. I was teaching a management development class. I thought I had been clear about the expectations. My role as teacher was to show up on time, to be prepared, and to let them out on time. Their role was to come to class on time, to take detailed notes, and to study for each class session.

We were in the third week of the course. As we reviewed the prior week's material, it was clear that nobody had studied. When I realized they had not studied, I said, "I assume you've had a busy week and have not been able to study. It's not beneficial to you to have another class until you have time to catch up. So class is dismissed, and I'll be prepared to teach when you learn the material from last week."

Well, what do you suppose happened the next week? A few people didn't show up. They wanted nothing else to do with class. That was fine. They weren't learning anything anyway. But the ones who did show up knew the material and knew it well.

I had previously taught a class at a church but didn't follow this approach. People fell behind and didn't know the material from the prior week, and I just let it go. It was no doubt the weakest class I ever taught. I wasted my time, and they wasted theirs.

When I dismissed the second class and made it clear people were to show up having learned the material from the prior week, everyone who came kept up. If students had been allowed to stay without being prepared, they would have adversely affected the rest of the class. They would have thought it was acceptable to come to class unprepared. As it worked out, the best got better and the weakest links in the chain were plenty strong.

This became one of the best classes I ever taught. And most of the people in that class got promoted one or more times in the next ten years.

How do people judge what you expect?

I once had a boss who had a new idea every week. If I thought it was a good idea, I did it immediately. If not, I waited. If he mentioned it again and it was an OK idea, I worked it in. If I thought it was a bad idea, I waited for him to mention it a third time before I discussed it with him and acted on it. Most of the ideas were never acted on because he never mentioned them twice or followed up.

Some leaders say people will do what you expect. I agree with that, and I've seen it many times. Other leaders believe people do what you inspect. I agree with that, and I've seen it many times. They aren't mutually exclusive theories. People tend to judge your true expectations based on your follow-up and focus. Having a lot of expectations without clear, consistent follow-up appropriate for the circumstances and individuals will generally result in less effectiveness in meeting expectations.

Does measuring guarantee progress?

Measuring something doesn't necessarily guarantee progress toward the objective. I learned by experience that just measuring without follow-up and accountability doesn't produce a result.

A common mistake leaders make is having too many expectations and too little follow-up. If I focused on variances between expectations and performance and required written action plans to close the gap, substantial improvement occurred. Often, all I had to do was say we needed to pay attention to a particular issue or the next step would be written action plans. People hated to write action plans. Many times, they would take action to close the gap before we got to that step.

Chapter 5 – Progress Through Enabling Control Systems

Application

I. Are you careful to make sure your expectations are understood when you delegate? Yes____ No____

II. Would your employees agree? Yes____ No____

III. Do you follow-up at reasonable intervals on your expectations?

Yes____ No____

IV. What changes do you need to make based on this chapter?

_____
_____
_____
_____
_____
_____
_____

Notes

Chapter 6

PROGRESS THROUGH MEASUREMENT

Thought:
How much easier would your work be and how much more in control would you feel if you had a few measurable indicators telling you what you need to know?

"Immediately the one who had received the five talents went and traded them, and gained five more."

Matthew 25:16

Empowering Progress

We like to keep score. We can't go to a kids T-ball game, where the score is not officially kept, and not try to keep up with it in our heads. Keeping score gives us a sense of accomplishment. Would you keep playing golf if you couldn't keep score? Would you keep watching sports if scores weren't kept? Of course not. We have an innate need to create and be productive. Keeping score lets us know how we're doing. Measuring and reporting the right things can have substantial impact on the progress of an organization. Measuring the wrong things can hurt an organization.

Jack Welch once said at an HCA leadership conference, "If you can't measure it, you can't manage it." That's certainly true for organizations. It impacts people if you measure key performance indicators, communicate the measurements, and follow up on them. The key is what to measure. Put simply, you measure the high priorities—those things that move the needle.

Scripture says God numbers the hairs on my head. We are enough like our Creator that built within us is the desire to keep score. I know some people in ministry who give the impression that keeping score is bad. Yet these people are like all the other parents at the kids' T-ball games. They know if their team won. Imagine going to a football game or basketball game and not keeping score. How much fun would any sports activity be if scores were not kept? Have you noticed how frequently the score of the game is displayed on the TV screen?

Chapter 6 – Progress Through Measurement

I will be the first to acknowledge that keeping score can be done wrongly and cause damage. Yet in the parable of the talents, score was kept and the stewards were rewarded for multiplying their investments. Peter asked Jesus what he and others would get for forsaking all and following Him. Jesus did not rebuke him. Instead, He said a hundred times what he had given up. If we are keeping score only to show that we beat someone else, perhaps that is unhealthy competition. But in Scripture, accomplishment is commanded, commended, and rewarded.

So, how do we keep score in organizations? An organization has measures it tracks daily, weekly, monthly, and annually. It knows exactly where it stands against expectations for those timeframes. How about the employees? Do they know how they're doing within defined time intervals? If you don't keep score and provide feedback, they are likely to experience some anxiety or insecurity that is not necessary if they are doing well.

You may say, "We can't measure everything we want the employee to accomplish." This is particularly true in certain complex leadership roles. You can, however, give feedback on as much objective data as possible as well as your perspective on performance versus expectations. Lee Iacocca did this quarterly with his vice presidents when he turned Chrysler around.

I adopted the same approach at the vice president level in my organizations and believed it added to the focus and accomplishment and contributed to a lack of surprises or disappointments in the annual review process. The frequency of feedback depends on the role, concrete data that may be available, and the personality of the individual. Some people like broad measures over longer periods of time. Others tend to need more frequent feedback and affirmation.

What should we try to impact?

What we should measure is tied to the mission, values, vision, and priorities of the organization. We should measure things that directly relate to these, and special focus should be placed on priorities that have been agreed upon for the next year. When establishing measures, keep in mind what really "moves the needle." You're far better off narrowing your focus and measuring a few key things that contribute most toward your vision. Think about how a river works. The narrower the banks are, the faster the water flows.

One mistake leaders sometimes make is failing to have balanced measures. If we measure quantity but not quality, we tend to produce poor quality goods or services. If we only measure quality but not quantity, we tend to be less productive. If our focus is only on cost and trying to reduce it, we may negatively impact quality.

I've seen numerous examples of new initiatives in organizations where measures are not kept in balance. One company did a massive computer conversion where the information technology department was incentivized based on the number of conversions but not the quality or the downstream costs to the revenue cycle of a poor conversion.

In Physician Services, as we rolled out new service lines, we had to balance the speed and quality of the program. There were times where hospital or division operators wanted something done very quickly. Responding to those requests and doing things more quickly than we knew was prudent always caused problems that we had to fix. In the end, it took longer than doing it right in the first place.

Often, our leadership in Physician Services found themselves working hard to put the brakes on programs so we could implement them at a speed that would not create additional problems.

Micromanagers versus control systems

Leaders of small organizations tend to limit the activity of their organizations to what they can personally oversee. One reason they want to be so personally engaged is to have a sense of control. Yet a clearly-established, measurable standard and a reporting system to identify progress and exceptions give leaders much more control than mere personal oversight does.

That doesn't mean "management by walking around" isn't a good idea. It is. Leaders' walking around and observing are informal acts of measurement. Plus, there are benefits to the leaders' being engaged beyond the measurement and control system aspect.

The chain is no stronger than its weakest link

I saw this principle applied at HCA one time in the area of accounts receivable. As a company, the days of accounts receivable were just too high. The average for the company was in the seventy to eighty range. Leadership thought fifty-five was a reasonable standard. So they printed stickers and created banners that said, *"Stay alive at 55."* But what began to change things was the publishing of results and comparison of the operating units. Now that there was a contest, about 10% of the business office managers in the company wanted to have the lowest days of accounts receivable. So they started working on ways to improve the results. And they did. After eighteen months, the top business office managers had their days of accounts receivable average less than forty.

What about the other business office manager? Well, some of them began to learn from those who had better results. So their days in accounts receivable went down. In some divisions, training programs were implemented and several of the business office managers improved their results. In some cases, business office managers were not able to learn enough from others or the training programs to improve the results. Some looked for easier jobs, and others were asked to leave.

Here was the dynamic I observed. When the worst days in receivable in a division were ninety, the office manager at eighty or eighty-five was comfortable. When the worst came down to their level, they got really busy looking for ways to improve. The end result after eighteen months was that the worst hospital was at fifty-five days, and the company average was about forty-seven.

So let's make application to organizational life. Who sets the performance standard? Most operating managers quickly say management does. I ask, "How?" They say, "We set the performance goals and standards." I ask, "Are they always met?" Rarely does anyone ever say yes. So I ask again, "Then who is setting the standard?" The real answer is the "weakest link in the chain." It is the people known to have the lowest level of performance who continue to keep their jobs in the organization. As long as everyone else can look at those people and know they're doing better, they feel safe. And that is fine as long as those people's level of performance is acceptable.

The bottom line is: to get improvement, do these things:

- Measure and publish results;
- Create a contest where the top performers can compete;
- Create opportunities for the lowest performers to learn from others;
- Offer training to help people meet the performance standards; and
- Make a change in personnel if people are not qualified for the job.

Application

I. Do you measure things related to the mission, vision, values, and priorities in your organization?

Yes____ No____

What are the five things you could measure to maximize your organization's impact?

1._____
_____

2._____
_____

3._____
_____

4._____
_____

5._____
_____

II. Do you share measures with the team so they can see how they are doing relative to their goals and relative to their peers?

Yes____ No____

Notes

Part II

II. POWER

"For even the Son of Man did not come to be served, but to serve, and to give his life a ransom for many."

Mark 10:45

"But the greatest among you shall be your servant."

Matthew 23:11

"But it is not this way with you, but the one who is the greatest among you must become like the youngest, and the leader like the servant."

Luke 22:26

Questions to Ponder

- What is power?

- What is your attitude toward power?

- Do you wish you had more influence on other people?

- Do you understand the difference between positional power and real, lasting power?

- Do you know the key to becoming a leader and staying a leader?

INTRODUCTION TO POWER

We all want progress in our organizations, but progress has to be empowered. As leaders think about power, there are two key decisions they have to make. One is their attitude toward power. Why do they want it? Many people want power to be able to control people and events. To them, it's about control and ego. The more people they can control and the more they can control them, the better they feel about themselves. They feel strong and safe.

Then there are those who want power to be able to make life better for others. They express confidence in the people around them and share power with them. They may establish control systems, but their primary aim is not to control other people.

The controlling leader tends to be a micromanager. He or she wants to make all the detail decisions and tends to look over people's shoulders. Control systems are established more to keep people in line than to guide and protect.

By contrast, the leader who wants to serve shares power with the team. How do they do this? We will discuss it later in more detail. But in general terms, the vision of a servant leader is translated into priorities. Those priorities are expressed in individual goals. The goals are given to people with the talent and the desire to achieve them. Finally, there is an accountability and control system to keep people on track with the goals to which they agree. They continually know where they stand.

Notes

Chapter 7

ABUSING POWER

> **Thought:**
> Have you considered how much you damage your organization and hurt yourself when you abuse power?

"He spoke to them according to the advice of the young men saying, 'My father made your yoke heavy, but I will add to it; my father disciplined you with whips, but I would discipline you with scorpions.'"

2 Chronicles 10:14

> *"You know that the rulers of the Gentiles lord it over them, and their great men exercise authority over them. It is not that way among you, but whoever wishes to become great among you shall be your servant..."*
>
> *Matthew 20:25-26*

As we think about power, let's think first about how not to use it. My desire for the wrong kind of power came when I was just a boy. I've abused it and learned a valuable lesson. I tend to think abuse of power starts very early in life with others too. We either grow beyond it or stay trapped in it.

I was raised on a small farm, for which I'm grateful. We had dairy cows but also raised hogs to sell. The hogs were a problem. They tended to get outside the fence and root the grass in our fields. So Daddy bought and installed an electric fence. He would test to see if the electric fence was working by taking a shovel, sticking it in the ground, and leaning the metal part against the fence. When it was working, it would create a small spark.

Sometimes, when we fed the hogs, some grains of corn would fall close to or under the electric fence. The hogs would touch the fence, get shocked, squeal, and jump back. As a kid, I thought that was funny. Sometimes I would drop kernels of corn leading up to the fence, knowing the hogs would focus on the corn and touch the fence. It worked 100% of the time. They always went after the corn and hit the fence. I wasn't doing it to be mean. I just thought it was funny.

Then I decided to escalate the game. I tied a string to an ear of corn. The hogs would go for it, and I would pull the corn toward the fence. In going for the corn, two or three hogs would touch the fence, squeal, and jump back. I felt smart, in control, and it seemed funny to me.

I got creative and decided to escalate the game again. I climbed to the top of a small shed which was about nine feet high. I tied an ear of corn to a string and lowered it to the ground. The hogs would go for it, and I would pull it just out of their reach. They would chase it, and I would continually pull it just out of their reach. That was entertaining for a while. Then, I decided I wanted to see if I could make them dance. So when they were fully engaged in going for that piece of corn, I lifted it just above their heads. They would stand on their hind legs snapping at the ear of corn. I had made them dance!

Sometimes they would get the ear of corn in their mouths, and I would jerk it out. A couple of times, they got a good hold on the corn and were able to jerk the string out of my hand. The string burned my hand. Plus, I had to climb off the roof to get the string again.

So I wrapped the string around my hand so that they wouldn't be able to jerk it out so easily. What happened next was rather predictable. I was confident they couldn't jerk the string from my hand, so I took a little more risk. I let them get the corn in their mouths and jerked it out. There was one five-hundred-pound hog that was standing straight up on her hind legs. She got the ear of corn locked firmly in the back part of her jaw. She flicked her big strong neck, and I came sailing off the roof like a small missile.

It had been a while since the last rain. So the once muddy hog lot now had dry, hard, lumpy clumps of dirt. As the hog dragged me across those rockhard lumps, my chest and groin area were catching the brunt of the punishment. Thank God, after a few yards, the string broke. The hog had the corn, and I was free.

The moral of the story

- It's not okay to have fun at another's expense, even if the other is a hog.

- When your goal is simply to entertain yourself, the game continues to escalate and the risk gets higher, and someone's going to get hurt.

- You will likely be the one that gets hurt the most.

At the point in this story where I said I wanted to make the pigs dance, was your first thought, "I wonder how he's going to make a pig dance?"

Or was your first thought, "Why would you want to make a pig dance?" You see, *why* I wanted to make a pig dance showed a lot about my motives. I wanted power and control. I wanted to be entertained at the pig's expense. That was wrong, and it was costly.

Application to corporate life

I thought of this experience on more than one occasion in corporate meetings. I saw sophisticated, educated, polished, professional managers (notice I said managers, not leaders) at times do the same thing I did with hogs at nine years old. These people were supposed to be mature adults. And to be honest, there were times when I was tempted to or did play the game again with people. So what does this look like a corporate life?

First, executives forget the primary purpose they are to be serving. They begin to think about a game to be played rather than a purpose to be served, a mission to be achieved, or a vision to be realized.

Next, they begin to entertain themselves at other people's expense. This causes anxiety, confusion, and sometimes deep emotional pain. But that's okay with these leaders because they see the people they are impacting as lesser beings to be toyed with.

Then comes boredom with the game, and it escalates. The managers must show their superiority, their higher intelligence, and finally their power over others. These insensitive, immature, and ego driven executives are going to win a lot of the power games. Each time they win, they feel smarter, more secure, more powerful, and more invincible. Thus, they take greater and greater risks.

Finally, they start to believe they can't lose. But they have grossly underestimated the power of the opposing force. They are jerked hard from their pedestals. They're not like I was—a poor farm boy who could only afford a grass string from a bale of hay rather than a rope that wouldn't break. These people are locked in with metaphorical triple-cord rope, and they are metaphorically dragged as far as their opposers wants to drag them. It's an ugly sight.

The last thing they see is the gleam in their opposer's eye that says, "I got you now." Believe it or not, I saw the same gleam in that hog's eye just before she flicked her neck and jerked me from the roof. I've seen this many times in corporate life and in nonprofit organizations and ministries. I've seen many professionals jerked from their pedestals like human missiles. The lessons are the same.

- Our work has a purpose that should be taken seriously.

- Others are not there for our entertainment or sport.

- When you start entertaining yourself, the game escalates, and someone's going to get hurt.

- You will hurt many others along the way.

- You may very well be the one most hurt in the end.

Application

I. Do you pit people against one another in your organization?

Yes_____ No_____

II. Do you try to manipulate and control your people?

Yes_____ No_____

III. Do you at times see organizational life as a game?

Yes_____ No_____

IV. What changes do you need to make so you don't hurt yourself or others?

_____
_____
_____
_____
_____
_____
_____
_____

Chapter 7 – Abusing Power

V. Do you give power away routinely, i.e., empower people, or do you hang on to power?   Give it away_____   Keep it_____

If you tend to try to keep it, what changes will you make?

_____
_____
_____
_____
_____
_____
_____

Notes

Chapter 8

A MODEL SURE TO FAIL – MICROMANAGING

> **Thought:**
> Do you have any idea how much productivity and morale are lost by your micromanagement?

"Then the Lord God took the man and put him into the Garden of Eden to cultivate it and keep it. The Lord commanded the man, saying, 'From any tree of the garden you may freely; but from the tree of the knowledge of good and evil you shall not eat.'"

Genesis 2:15-16

Micromanaging is the antithesis of empowering people. People tend to see God as a micromanager. But the Scripture above shows what great freedom He gives people. The antithesis of using goals to lead an organization is the perfectionist-oriented leader. You may say, "Well, what's wrong with being a perfectionist? Don't you want things done right?" My answers used to be "nothing" and "yes" respectively, but I have come to understand than perfectionist tendencies can be a great weakness in leading people. You can't get or keep the best people with this approach. Certain personality profiles tend to be perfectionist-oriented. For example, the "C" competent/compliant profile tends toward perfectionism. Real leadership and micromanagement are at opposite ends of the spectrum. Micromanagement has no rightful place in the life of a leader.

The effects of micromanagement

What's the problem of being a perfectionist manager? Notice again that I said manager, not leader. Such managers tend to want to control people and processes. Leaders cast vision, attract people to it, and help set priorities and strategies. Perfectionist managers pick at small things; employees get focused on lesser priorities.

Remember the 80/20 rule. Not all tasks are of equal value. Make sure the 20% of tasks that drive 80% of results get the focus. When you start focusing on the 80%, that only drives 20% of the results and requires perfection that disorients and actually detracts from employees' staying focused on the real priorities.

Chapter 8 – A Model Sure to Fail – Micromanaging

God is a God of order, not of chaos. God is not a micromanager. He holds people accountable, but He does not micromanage their daily lives. When managers nitpick, they create confusion for employees or volunteers. They disorient some. They frustrate them. They throw them off track. And over time, they cause them to be less effective in their jobs. But don't misapply this. Some things have to be perfect—like health care and air travel.

What do you do if you are a perfectionist leader?

Being aware of your perfectionist tendencies is a good first step. Controlling those tendencies and avoiding them in your leadership style is the next step.

I had an extremely capable executive administrative assistant. There was always a lot going on, and I delegated a lot of work to her. Being so conscientious, she wanted to do it all and wanted to do it well. Being perfectionist-oriented, I wanted it all done and done well. I had to remind myself to communicate with her daily about the high priorities. I would say, "Here's why they are priorities. Do these first. Do these well. Do these other items when you have time. They don't have to be perfect." This kept the focus on the priorities. When I did this, it took a lot of pressure off my assistant.

Having high expectations is fine. Adhering to high quality standards is good. In the airline industry and the healthcare industry, lives are at stake if quality standards are not maintained. I'm not talking about ignoring quality standards. I'm talking about not "nitpicking" employees about low priority activities.

What if I work for a perfectionist-oriented leader?

I had one boss who was perfectionist-oriented. He wanted it all done and done at a high level of quality. When I saw it was not possible to do everything at quality standards, I would proactively go to him and ask about the priorities to make sure we stayed in sync. I never had a time when he wasn't glad to discuss priorities. Actually, 100% of the time he told me not to worry about the lesser priority items. That gave me freedom to focus on the high priority items and let the lower priority items go.

Example

I've had both the pleasure and the challenge of working with a number of doctors. While very intelligent and gifted, their training and the practice of medicine causes many of them to be perfectionist-oriented. This is great when practicing medicine, but not so great when trying to lead a physician practice as it grows. For example, one practice had some computer-related issues that occurred several times during the year. Due to a micromanaged task reporting system, the team would report on each instance of the problem and what they did to get the system working again. They reported the same issue numerous times and looked very productive. However, a more effective, results-oriented solution would have been to identify the root cause of the problem, set a timeframe for resolving it, and report the resolution at the appropriate time. The question is this: Are you focused on achieving results over time, or are you focused on people reporting on tasks more frequently?

Application

I. Do you have perfectionist tendencies? Yes____ No____

What changes do you need to make so that you don't confuse your team?

_____
_____
_____
_____
_____
_____
_____
_____

II. Do you work for a perfectionist? Yes____ No____

What changes will you make in your approach to dealing with that person?

_____
_____
_____
_____
_____
_____

Empowering Progress

Chapter 9

WHAT IS REAL POWER?

> **Thought:**
> How much would you enjoy your work if people did what you asked willingly and eagerly, without grumbling or complaint?

"...The Son of Man did not come to be served, but to serve, and to give his life a ransom for many."
Matthew 20:28

- Do you have as much influence as you want?
- Do you know healthy ways to influence others?
- Do you use destructive approaches to influence others?
- Do you know the difference?

Power can be a great thing or terrible thing, depending on whether it is used constructively or destructively. Great power rests in the hands of leaders in organizational life.[1] I've seen it used for great good and, sadly, I've seen it used many times with destructive effects. I've see this in business organizations, nonprofit organizations, ministries, and churches.

Empowering progress

From traveling in Europe and hearing the history, I get a clear perspective of attitudes toward power. These countries were lead for much of their history by dictators who were all about controlling people and events for their interests or pleasures. There is a radical difference between this and empowering people in healthy organizations to achieve goals to which they've agreed toward visions they want to help accomplish.

WHAT IS POWER?

Power is the possibility to influence others.[2] It is clear that leaders have power and the ability to use that power for great good. You may say, "I want to be a leader and have power so I can make a difference." That's a worthy ambition. So how do you become a leader? How do you stay a leader? What makes a leader different from other people? What do leaders have that others don't? You may say intelligence, good looks, or high-energy. Jim Collins refuted all that in his description of "level five" leaders.[3] I've seen people with all these traits who weren't great leaders. I have also seen examples of people with none of these who were.

Why did people follow Jesus? Peter followed Jesus at least in part because He appealed to the "I" portion of Peter's personality when He promised to make him a fisher of men. Judas obviously followed Jesus because he wanted access to power and wealth. He thought Jesus would be a political and military leader and would overthrow the Roman government. He wanted to be part of the reigning class. Part of James and John's motivation for following Jesus was that they thought He would grant them desirable positions in heaven. They wanted to occupy the thrones to the left and right of Him in heaven. Their mother wanted the same for them. The bottom line is that everybody who followed Jesus expected something from Him.

In pursuing what they perceive as best for themselves, people pick leaders throughout their lives to follow. The people they follow are not always good people. They do not always lead to good results. They are not always good-looking, caring, or even intelligent. They are simply people followers think will do something for them.

WHAT IS YOUR ATTITUDE TOWARD POWER?

Let's look at power from a biblical perspective. At the time Jesus entered human history, people understood power based on the system of kings and emperors they were accustomed to. These rulers had totalitarian control over people's lives. Their regimes most often were controlling, harsh, and corrupt. God's people were looking forward to a Messiah who would come as an earthly king and be a military and political leader. They expected Him to overthrow the Roman government and exercise power for the benefit of the nation of Israel. When He came as a servant leader and said, "I came not to be served, but to serve and give my life as a ransom for many," this mystified the people. This was not how a king thought and acted, at least not any king they had seen.

Jesus had no intention of governing as a totalitarian leader. He would not force people to follow Him. They would follow Him out of choice based on the gratitude and love they had for him because of His sacrifice on their behalf. In Revelation 3:20, He says, "Behold, I stand at the door knock and if anyone will open the door I will come in and eat with him and he with me." Notice that Jesus never forces His way into anyone's life. He initiates the relationship but waits for the invitation to come into a person's life. He asks for complete surrender, but it's based on the person's loving choice to follow Him willingly, not by force.

Jesus was the perfect example of a servant leader. Think about the example He gave us. He created everything. Then, He left heaven, where He had no limits, to take on the limits of the human body. The creator of the universe became a carpenter to make a living for His family. He taught and served His disciples and others throughout His ministry. Then He gave His life on the cross in excruciating pain and humiliation so that we could have a relationship with God.

People want a king

As we search Scripture further, we see that people in the time of Jesus were the same as people thousands of years earlier. Right after the time of the judges in the Old Testament, the people asked God for a king. This was when Samuel judged Israel and felt like the people were rejecting him as leader. God told Samuel it was God Himself they were rejecting. They did not want God to rule over them (1 Samuel 8:10-18). Scripture says they wanted somebody that would fight the battles for them and protect them. God warned them about the future consequences, but they ignored those warnings.

It was my personal experience in thirty-five years of leadership that people still want protection and someone to fight their battles for them. And they want provision. People will gladly follow leaders who will do those things for them.

Leadership choices

This review of Scripture gives us two clear choices. Are we going to rule like ancient kings, the autocratic, controlling, and sometimes abusive, totalitarian leaders? Or are we going to lead like Jesus? Will we lead as servants? Will we train, mentor, and empower people the way Jesus did, or will we abuse them?

Temporary power vs. lasting power

The tyrants of long ago had great power because of their totalitarian governments. Their power was temporary however. People stopped following them when they no longer held office. With Jesus, in contrast, the disciples followed Him wholeheartedly all of their lives—freely and by choice. Disciples today still follow Jesus in this manner. Would you rather have a workforce that follows you because they want to or because they feel like they have to? Which type of followers will serve your customers and constituents best over time? Which one will be the best to lead and work with? Which one do you want to be associated with? How do you want to be viewed as a leader—tyrant or servant? Robert K. Greenleaf and others have written much about servant leadership in our generation. There are numerous books on the subject. Yet we need to look no further than the scriptural examples of Moses, Nehemiah, the Apostle Paul and, for the ultimate example, Jesus Himself.

WHAT IS YOUR APPROACH TO POWER?

Will you use people or engage them? In my early years, I approached power from the perspective of using people to achieve worthwhile projects. I was not focused on blessing people by engaging them in worthwhile projects that they had the passion, personality, and preparation to help accomplish. This latter approach reminds me of King Solomon in the Old Testament. A visiting queen from a foreign country noticed how happy and blessed the people were under Solomon's leadership (though sadly, Solomon later failed miserably). I'm reminded of Nehemiah and how the people joined together and said, "Let us rebuild the wall." They had a shared vision, and everyone had a part of it. This stands in stark contrast to "We've got a big job; let's get to it" or "That's what we get paid for" or "If you can't get it done, I will find someone who will."

The key to blessing people with your power is rooted in Scripture—loving your neighbor as yourself, as Jesus said, or thinking of others and not just yourself, as Paul said.

When I got my spiritual attitude right, I began to think differently about how I engaged with people. I changed from seeking to control them and gettting them to do what I wanted to empowering them to do things they wanted to do that helped achieve the vision. There's a big difference in the attitude and output of people when they are complying with you rather than cooperating with you. When they are doing what they want to do, they have energy and passion.

DO YOU HAVE TO BE A "TOUGH GUY" TO LEAD?

There is a widely held perception today that a leader has to be a "tough guy" to be taken seriously. Otherwise, as the perception goes, you are seen as weak and unable to lead. This is the way many people see Jesus as a leader: weak and passive. This is not what I see at all when I take a close look at His leadership. He had many enemies, but He was not fearful or anxious. Many tried to trick Him, but He always had an appropriate answer and never lost a debate. He was kind and gentle to the sick, the disadvantaged, and, in general, the underdog. Yet He was bold with the religious leaders of His day. He called them "whitewashed tombs" (Matthew 23:25). He rebuked them publicly. He overturned the tables of the moneychangers in the temple, single-handedly driving them out.

These instances are not when He was the strongest though. The Apostle Paul said, "When I am weak then I am strong" (2 Corinthians 12:10). Jesus was strongest when He appeared the weakest. For example, when He was in the Garden of Gethsemane praying and sweating, He still mustered the courage and self-control to yield His will to God. When the centurions came for Him, He did not run or resist arrest. Instead, He was strong enough to forgive His enemy Judas, kiss him, and call him "friend." When he faced Pilate, he did not feel the need to defend Himself or try to talk Himself out of a horrible situation. He did not defend Himself in front of the people either. But where His strength was most revealed, in apparent weakness, was when He allowed Himself to be beaten, stripped, have thorns placed on His head, and be crucified without opposition. Remember Christ said He could call down ten legions of angels to protect Himself. Yet He was strong enough to suffer wrongfully and horribly without exercising any of His rights as an innocent man, much less the rights He had as the Creator and only Son of God.

There are a lot of benefits in not trying to be the "tough" corporate leader. Your best people stay with you. People cooperate with you rather than simply complying. People follow willingly rather than being manipulated. Other people are drawn to your culture so that you have your choice of the best people at all times. By contrast, the really tough leaders burn people out. Their people operate in cultures of fear, don't take risks, and are, therefore, less proactive. They leave when they get a chance. Other good people are not attracted to such cultures. I have seen those cultures sustain themselves for fairly long periods of time as long, as there are enough financial incentives to keep the people. But when those cords are cut, people will jump ship very quickly.

Nehemiah

Some leaders fear that if they soften their approaches with the team and do things through spiritual means, they will be seen as spiritual but not strong leaders. Most of us have the view that being a strong leader means being tough with people. That's not the case at all. To be an effective leader, we have to make tough decisions but seldom do we need to flex our muscles with the team. Nehemiah is a perfect example. When he went to Jerusalem to be the governor, he didn't exert himself and his power. Rather, he rallied the people around a vision so they, with one voice, said, "Let us rebuild the wall." (Later, he did have to challenge some of the people about how they were not living out God's Word by mistreating the poor, and he did not shy away from the issue. Instead, he guided the people to make the right decision.) I learned by experience that I had the most power when I thought about the team and what was best for them and the company, ignoring the impact on me personally.

Notes

Chapter 10

HOW TO BECOME A LEADER

> **Thought:**
> Are you a leader, manager, or supervisor?
> Do you know the difference?

Maybe you remember Dale Carnegie saying that "you can achieve any goal or dream you have if you're willing to help enough other people achieve their goals." Or maybe you remember the words of Jesus who said:

> *"It is not this way among you,*
> *but whoever wishes to become great among you shall be your servant, and whoever wishes to be first among you shall be your slave; just as the Son of Man did not come to be served, but to serve..."*
> *Matthew 20:26-27*

> *"But the greatest among you shall be your servant."*
> *Matthew 23:11*

> *"I came not to be served*
> *but to offer my life as a ransom for many."*
> *Mark 10:45*

I recently had a social lunch with the leader of a large privately-owned physician practice. He had just fired one of the doctors in the practice. This doctor had chewed out one of the support staff for scheduling a patient that was not convenient for him. He told this person never to schedule people at inconvenient times. Many doctors I know are compassionate and considerate of other peoople's needs. But there are some who do not have a selfless/servant heart.

Jesus' own people rejected Him because He was not the political, military leader they expected, who would exert power and control over people. When He led and died as a servant to rescue His people, they just didn't understand it. And many today still do not understand it. The purest form of power is when people follow you because they want to. People do what you say out of **force** or **choice**. They follow out of choice with their hearts. When they are forced to comply, they do so out of fear.[4] Only one is lasting. When the fear is gone, people no longer follow out of force. They will always follow when their allegiance stems from choice. In Revelation 3:20, Jesus makes it clear He does not force His way into people's lives or override their wills. He wants people to follow Him by choice, not by force.

<u>Standing on Faith</u>

How about us? As leaders, are we able and willing to be misunderstood, rejected, ridiculed, and humiliated without having to defend ourselves or our reputations? Are we willing to sacrifice for the good of others or even suffer for the good of others if it comes to it?

There is a strong perception among many who want to be leaders in the business and nonprofit sectors that they must fit in to get ahead. They are afraid to speak up for their faith, thinking they will be seen as weak and be bypassed for promotions. Scripture shows this isn't true. Joseph was upfront about his faith and was ultimately promoted everywhere God placed him, including prison. Nehemiah was a captive in a pagan kingdom. But he was open about his faith and became cupbearer for the king, one of the most important positions in the kingdom, and the person the king trusted the most in the entire kingdom. Daniel was also a Jewish captive serving a pagan king and, again, a person upfront about his faith. He was promoted above all the king's other assistants and highly regarded by the king. In fact, his integrity and devotion to God were the only faults the jealous bureaucrats in the kingdom could find in him.

STRONG THROUGH SERVICE

Early in my career, I led more like the "tough guy." Then I transitioned more to the other end of the spectrum, though I was never satisfied I had arrived. Early on, I was working, striving, and competing to get ahead in my career. I did, but it was hard on me and hard on others. I discovered that I got ahead most when I quit trying to get ahead and simply tried to serve the company well and help my team progress. I realized that leading God's way makes you a stronger leader. It also helps you grow spiritually. Here are some of the changes I made and how I grew spiritually when I quit worrying about me and started helping others get promoted:

From controlling to empowering

Because of my natural personality profile, my training as an accountant, and further development as an auditor, I was strongly oriented toward controlling everything. I wanted to do too much myself. I had a hard time letting go and even found it difficult to take vacations because I did not feel in control. I saw many examples in HCA of effective leaders who empowered others and had good accountability systems. I learned from them and began to empower people. I gave them substantial freedom coupled with accountability. My people liked it better, and it was an entirely different life for me. I grew spiritually by moving from pride and thinking I knew best to counting on and engaging others. I went from autocratic announcements to truly engaging people. In fact, in the last chapter of my career, I can barely think of any initiative or project of significance my team pursued that was my idea originally. All the best ideas came from the team in group brainstorming sessions.

From achieving my goals to serving the company well and helping other people achieve their goals

I remember reaching a significant marker in my career and thinking, "Now, what's next?" The problem was there wasn't any other position that I found exciting. What I did find exciting was deciding to help as many other people as I could to achieve their career ambitions and serve the company well. I quit thinking solely about what made my job easiest or made me look best as the leader. Instead, I focused on what was best for the company and what was best for each individual that I was entrusted to lead and train. When I did this, I did a much better job for the company, was appreciated much more by my people, found greater satisfaction and joy in my work, and was given opportunities to do things in the company beyond what I ever thought possible.

In hindsight, that seems so clear and right. But I remember how hard it was many times. I gave up key people to other parts of the company, which was best for the company and best for those individuals. But it left me scrambling and re-training to try to replace them. The people using the "tough guy" approach in the company restricted people from being promoted outside their functions or divisions, or at least strongly discouraged it. Over time, their people began to resent it, and certainly it was not best for the company. It takes strength to let somebody leave who is a key member of your team. It only takes selfishness to prohibit them. The strongest leader is one who can let go, not the one who can hold on the tightest or longest. I learned after the fact that God has a pleasant reward for those who can let go. When you get a reputation of doing what is best for people and for the company, the best people are willing to work with you and the company trusts you with greater levels of service. You see, I got what I had been striving for earlier and achieved it at much greater levels when the focus was not on me but on others.

From taking the company line to advocating for employees while supporting the company

Rules, policies, and procedures exist for a reason. Certainly as an auditor, I knew that. But the rules just don't make sense in certain instances for individuals and, therefore, are not in the best long-term interests of the company. "Tough guys" tend to use the policies to give them power. It takes a stronger person to challenge the policies and advocate for an individual when you know that's the right thing to do. Often, the people you are opposing made the policies and could use them against you later if you made them mad. Enforcing policies doesn't make you strong. Going against them when you know it is the right thing to do is what requires real strength.

From just doing my job to getting out of my box

In doing my job, I often did what the Bible would call "going the extra mile." Yet, I mostly did that either out of fear, to get noticed, or to get a promotion. When I quit being preoccupied with receiving promotions and just looked for ways to serve the company, I worked outside the box that my role called for at times. Sometimes that makes bureaucrats in the organization mad. Sometimes it's risky because you can be blamed if your endeavors don't go well. I used to think being in complete control of my assigned job was a sign of great strength. I later learned that venturing beyond my spot in the organizational chart to serve required more strength.

From trying to get recognition and credit to giving them to others

I think this was perhaps my most difficult lesson and one of the harder areas of spiritual growth to learn. We all seem to want the accolades of others. Proverbs 25:6 says, "Don't call attention to yourself in front of the King, but rather let others praise you." I can remember many times the team wanted me to do or say things to call attention to the department so we would get credit. But we learned by experience that taking on small initiatives and leading successful pilot projects was a better alternative. We would identify initiatives that we thought had potential. Then we would find a division willing to participate in a pilot. After the initiative succeeded, we would give them the credit and offer to help the next willing participant. We did this with several initiatives over the years. I can remember how hard it was to give others the credit, knowing we had started the project and done much of the work. Yet a pleasant surprise from God was in learning that, typically, the credit was merely deferred. Eventually, our contributions were recognized. In the boardroom, when somebody is praising you, that makes a much greater impact than if you grab the headlines yourself. Patience is one of the fruits of God's Spirit. It takes patience to wait for the credit you know is yours. It takes humility to wait and sometimes never receive the full credit that you know is yours. Both make you stronger and more durable in tough times.

From answering every criticism to taking it for what it was worth and trying to improve where I could

The typical "tough guy" has a response for every criticism and tries to put the critics back on their heels. I was especially prone to do this. It just seems like the thing a "tough guy" does. You don't let your opponent have the last word. Do you realize how much harder it is be criticized, say nothing, and simply learn from it—to see if there's any value in what is being said? Some of my greatest opportunities for spiritual growth and faith came from these experiences. My team would say, "Leon, you know that's not right. Why didn't you prove them wrong in front of the group? Why didn't you take up for yourself?" If it served some purpose, I did set the record straight and I did take up for the team. But there are times when you serve no purpose in defending yourself. When the truth comes out, people will respect you more for holding your tongue and not embarrassing them in a meeting. It takes more strength to do that than to "cut them off at the ankles" when you have the chance, though you may seem weak at the time.

Chapter 11

POWER OF POSITION VS. POWER OF SERVICE

Thought:
Do you get things done primarily by using your position?
Have you thought about the consequences?

Positional power, also called "legitimate power," is the power of an individual because of the relative position and duties of the holder of the position within the organization.[5]

In my positions at HCA, I had a great deal of what I will call "positional power"—sometimes called authority or formal power. It is derived from a person's position in the organization.[6] Because of my position, I could influence or require people to take certain actions. But I discovered after many years that the power I wanted most was not positional power. It was the power of having people follow me because they wanted to. Positional power stays with the position when you leave it. Real power goes with you wherever you are.[7]

Many times, people did not do what I asked or directed even though I had substantial positional power at the time. But also many times, people did what I asked even though I had no positional authority. I had helped them before. They knew I cared about them. They knew I would help them again.

The key to gaining followers

The bottom line is that if you want people to follow, you must help them achieve their goals. Notice that we keep coming back to the importance of individual goals. Claudia was one of the most capable people I ever hired. She was willing to work with me because I was able to convince her that HCA would help her reach her goals.

> *"Do not look out merely for your own interests.*
> *Look out for the interests of others."*
> *Philippians 2:4*

Selfless leaders

In a healthy organization, leaders look at their teams and try to figure out how to guide and support them.

Chapter 11 – Position of Power vs. Position of Service

> *"...that one wants to serve, to serve first. Then conscious choice brings one to aspire to lead."* [8]
>
> *"The work exists as much for the person as much as the person exists for the work."* [9]

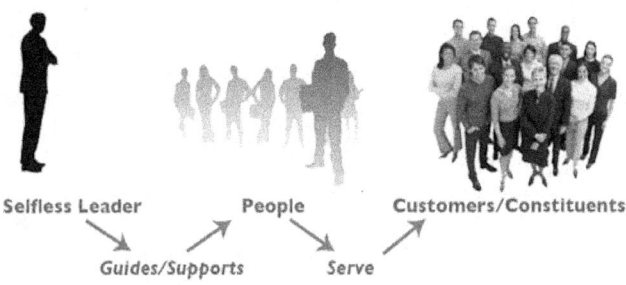

In this organization, all the people and activities are focused on providing a good or service to others. They look to the leader for purpose, vision, and support, but their daily focus is on providing a quality product or service.

Dr. Frist Sr.

Let me tell you a story about one of the three founders of HCA: Dr. Frist Sr. My aunt had been diagnosed with pancreatic cancer. She was in horrible pain and wanted a second opinion from a physician in Nashville. The family asked me who was best. At that time, I was a young executive and had no idea who she should see. I asked for an appointment with Dr. Frist Sr. My only goal was to ask him for the name or names of the best physicians for her to see.

He said, "Wait a minute" and quickly turned around and got a physician on the phone. He said, "I have someone I want you to see when are you available." It was Friday, and the physician apparently said Tuesday of the next week. I was traveling that week but learned that Dr. Frist Sr. met my aunt and family in the physician's lobby. He talked to them before and after they saw the doctor.

That's the kind of company I grew up in. Our founders were servant leaders. They had a heart and compassion for people. Work was never a game for them, and they took every day seriously. They made people's lives better, not worse. The remarkable thing about Dr. Frist Sr. is that this story is one of hundreds that could be told about him. I shared this one because it was my own experience.

Dr. Frist Sr. had a favorite saying: "Good people beget good people and bad people beget bad people." His point certainly holds true in organizational life. Good people know other good people and are able to attract them into the organization. Bad people know other bad people and tend to pull them into the organization. Again, this shows the vital importance of being diligent in hiring to make sure you have strong people with values aligned with those of the organization.

I learned through studying Jesus in the Scriptures and the lives of other role models that real, lasting power isn't what you claim or possess through positions of authority. It's the power people give you over their lives and actions because they believe you will help them. How do we use our power as leaders to most effectively serve people? We serve people by:

- Helping them set goals that give them a clear direction and sense of importance while helping the organization achieve its mission.

- Empowering them with systems, policies, and procedures that provide boundaries, but don't discourage them.

- Creating cultures conducive to energy and creativity.

Leaders who are secure in their relationships with God are able to serve better. When we find our identity in our relationships with God and live in the awareness that we are His sons and daughters, we don't have to strive for power. We don't have to compete to be better than other people. We realize He made us for a special purpose. We are not competing with anybody else to live out that purpose. That allows us to give power away. It allows us to serve well. We don't have to worry about image, reputation, or being better than someone else. We only need to focus on living out who we are and the purpose for which God created us.

Chapter 11 – Position of Power vs. Position of Service

Application

I. In what ways do your people need help?

_____
_____
_____
_____

II. Do you want to help them? Yes____ No____

If not, how can you cultivate a desire to help them?

_____
_____
_____
_____

III. Do they know you are willing to help them? Yes____ No____

If not, how will you inform them?

_____
_____
_____
_____

IV. Do you have people on your team that you have helped too much and that have become dependent on you? Yes_____ No_____

If yes, how can you rectify this situation?

_____
_____
_____
_____
_____
_____
_____

Chapter 12

THE APPROACH TO POWER – KEEP IT OR DISTRIBUTE IT

> **Thought:**
> Have you ever wondered why some businesses, churches, and other organizations seem to stay small while others tend to grow larger and larger?

"Then the Lord God took the man and put him in the Garden of Eden to cultivate it and keep it."

Genesis 2:15

Empowering Progress

I have noticed a tendency for small businesses to hit barriers and stay small. Nonprofit organizations spring up everywhere but only a few get large. There are several mega churches in the United States, but most churches are small, under one hundred people. Why is that? Why do so many businesses, churches, and other organizations tend to plateau and not grow any further? One key is how they approach the use of power. Are they going to approach it like Moses did at the beginning of his leadership of Israel? He kept all the power, and people gathered around him waiting for him to judge their cases and give them direction. Or are they going to approach it like Jethro suggested to Moses? That is, identify capable leaders, provide training, and empower them to act on most cases, keeping only the hardest cases for himself—management by exception.

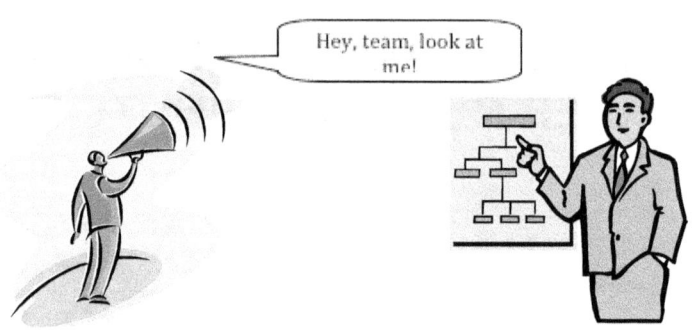

Today, we tend to refer to these two models, respectively, as the "mom and pop" or sole proprietor approach and the franchise approach to leadership and empowerment. I observed the former approach as I grew up in a small town at the local grocery and hardware stores. They had few employees, and everything revolved around the owner. HCA gave me the opportunity to experience a different style of leadership as is common in large companies and franchises. In the first approach, the power is retained by the owner, or the founder in a nonprofit organization or ministry. In the second, power is distributed to a number of other people. It works the same way in large, sophisticated organizations as it does in franchise organizations.

Chapter 12 – The Approach To Power

LIMITATIONS OF KEEPING THE POWER

One reason small businesses and organizations stay small is that the focus is on the owners/founders. They always have ownership and control of the organization. At some local businesses, the owner is always there making the decisions. When he's out, the employees have to call or wait for him to return before making a decision outside the norm.

When organizations are led this way, they never outgrow what the individual leaders can touch. What's the difference between a person owning and running one restaurant and the same person owning and running ten, twenty, thirty, or even one hundred restaurants? With some basic skills in the restaurant business, people can run a single restaurant. However, to run ten restaurants or one hundred, they have to approach it much differently, like a franchise. What makes franchises and large organizations like HCA different?

- Operating manuals for each key aspect of the organization indicating how things are to be done.

- Measurement of certain key activities and standards of what is expected.

- Checks and balances so that activities have an acceptable level of control but are not stifled.

- Information technology and management reporting so leaders can know what's going on without always being there physically to see and observe.

Franchises require goals for individual business units and goals, coupled with good training, for each position in the organization. They have great policy and procedure guides, operating manuals, training systems, and control systems. Managers are carefully selected and trained to operate successfully within acceptable boundaries.[10]

Empowering Progress

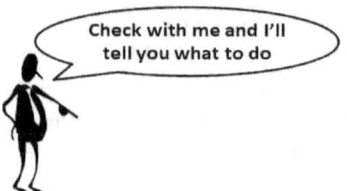

Sole Proprietor

Check with me and I'll tell you what to do

Note: When you keep power, everything revolves around you.

Franchise or large organization

Policies and Procedures, Operating Manuals, Training and Documentation

Vision & Goals

Enabling Control Systems

Note: When you give people power, goals give a strong sense of direction and freedom within the broad boundaries of policies and procedures. Goals are like the current of the river. Policies and procedures are like the banks of the river. They keep the flow consistent.

In franchise systems, the owners/leaders can't be in every restaurant every day. But when the operating parameters are properly established, levels of service quality and profitability can be consistently achieved. With good management-reporting systems and controls, the owners can know where each restaurant stands in a timely manner.

Large organizations are more sophisticated in using documentation, training, policies, and procedures to guide the organization. Small organizations tend to devote less time and energy to developing operating manuals, written policies and procedures, control systems, and management-reporting systems. They tend to accomplish things by the owner's/founder's individual engagement and oversight. Therefore, they can't grow beyond what the leaders can oversee personally.

EMPOWER PEOPLE LIKE FRANCHISES AND LARGE ORGANIZATIONS

In this model, like I experienced at HCA, goals are established with people. They are empowered to operate within those goals. There are policies and procedures in place to empower decision-making and to guide it. This model is not dependent on the leader's continual presence day to day for its functioning. People know what to do, how to do it, and are empowered within certain guidelines to take action. I experienced this the times I was out for extended periods of time.

Functioning without the leader present

I remember many years ago when the CEO of HCA had an accident which kept him out of work for several weeks. He came back and was pleasantly surprised at how well the company had done without him. But he also felt bad because it seemed like the team didn't need him in order to be successful. The truth was he was a great leader who had put in place the right team with the right policies, procedures, systems, and goals. And he had empowered them. His role was casting the vision and making sure the team grew and evolved to the vision. His role was not being involved in the details of day-to-day activities.

This man was an entrepreneurial leader who put a chief operating officer and others around him. He empowered them to run the day-to-day operations of the company. Of great significance, he was able to trust the people he put in place and let them do their jobs without interference. Failure of leaders to let go and trust others with the organization are two of the greatest obstacles I've seen to taking the organizations to the next level. HCA continued to prosper because its CEO had:

- Clear plans—mission, vision, and objectives;

- People in place with clear goals who agreed with the mission, vision, and values of the organization and were competent for their roles; and

- Control systems to keep things on track.

This discussion of large organizations versus small organizations does not mean large organizations are good and small organizations aren't. Often, people enjoy working in small organizations. They can also become very frustrated working in large, bureaucratic organizations, where policies and procedures can be constructed in ways that frustrate and cause anxiety. However, using these tools properly gives leaders great freedom and improves morale and productivity of the employees in both small and large organizations.

A small business owner makes the transition

I knew a man who was working seventy hours per week and felt incredibly frustrated much of the time. He had a profitable small business and was doing well financially but worn out from working so many hours. Then he implemented the franchise model of leadership over the course of a year. He was able to reduce his hours to thirty or forty per week with profitable results.

Early personal experience

Early in my career, I felt like I always had to be there to ensure everything was accomplished. I worked long hours five and six days a week. I never took the vacation time allotted each year. Once I learned how to employ the franchise model of leadership, that all changed. I took time off and didn't have to work as many hours.

Some years later, while I was in Physician Services, I had a major surgery and was out of the office for an extended period of time. I phased back in slowly, working two hours a day, then four, then six, and so on. Physician Services accomplished its goals just as well while I was gone as it did when I was there. So did I not matter? Well, if I had not gone back, there were many service lines, such as Anesthesia Services and Hospitalist Services, that never would have been developed. I helped create the vision and plans, staff the organization with the right leadership, and ensure systems and controls were created to run those lines of business. But I didn't have to daily manage the existing service lines.

I had a radical change in my view from early in my career when I felt I had to be there all the time to ensure that things ran well. I changed to the view that if I had to be there daily for things to run smoothly, I did not have it set up right. I came to view my role as that of visioning and

Chapter 12 – The Approach To Power

helping create the future with most of my time, and then being available to support the team with the rest of it. My goal was not to be needed on a day-to-day basis.

Application to nonprofits

Let us look at a biblical example: Moses. Even though he led a large number of people, he functioned mor like the new entrepreneurial leader. He cast the vision of freedom from Egypt and going to the Promised Land. Because of the miracles that God performed through him, the people eventually admired and followed him. Yet when it came to the day-to-day management of the people, he tried to function like small business owners, small church pastors, and small nonprofit directors. The first leadership consultant I see in the Bible was Jethro, Moses' father-in-law. He paid the family a visit out in the desert and observed. He noticed three things:

- Moses trying to do it all
- The stress and strain on Moses
- How tiresome it was for the people standing in line to wait for Moses' decision

Jethro said, in essence, "Moses, you need an organization, you need a system, and you need some guidelines and training programs for your leaders and people."

"The thing that you are doing is not good.
You will surely wear out, both yourself and these people who
are with you, for the task is too heavy for you; you cannot do it
alone."
Exodus 18:17-18

> *"Then teach them the statutes and the laws, and make known to them the way in which they are to walk and the work they are to do. Furthermore, you should select out of all the people able men who fear God, men of truth, those who hate dishonest gain; and you shall place these over them as leaders of thousands, of hundreds, 50s and tens.*
>
> *Let them judge the people at all times; and let it be that every major dispute they bring to you, but every minor dispute they themselves will judge. So it will be easier for you, and they will bear the burden with you. If you do this thing and God so commands you, then you will be able to endure, and all these people also will go to their place in peace. So Moses listened to his father-in-law and did all that he had said."*
>
> *Exodus 18:20-23*

He said, "You need to choose some leaders, and here are their qualifications. Put some in charge of thousands, some in charge of hundreds, and some in charge of fifties." Then, as now, choosing the right leaders to empower is key to the success of the organization. It's also key to taking the stress and strain off the top leader and making life better for all the people.

Jethro also said to Moses, "Assign the leaders and their teams, teach them the rules, and empower them to make decisions. Then, Moses, you only take the hard cases." This freed Moses up to spend time praying, thinking, and planning so he could keep the vision before the people and make wise decisions rather than being worn out and wearing the people out who were waiting on him.

Blessing people by empowering them

How are people blessed in organizations that empower them? First of all, they are freed to pursue clear goals and are empowered to act without always being told what to do or someone always looking over their shoulder.

Chapter 12 – The Approach To Power

I remember one of my direct reports, who lived out of state, saying he had received four emails from me in two years and all of those were responses to his emails. He said, "I don't think I could ever accuse you of micromanaging." This was a very capable leader who had a clear set of goals. All he needed from me was occasional support and occasional discussion to answer a question.

God instilled a need for freedom in people. He runs the universe by giving people clear directions. He gave an operating manual, the Bible, to guide and instruct us. And the Holy Spirit is available for day-to-day, specific guidance. God gives His people a great deal of freedom but with guidance and accountability.

People like freedom, need freedom, and seek freedom. God gave man great freedom when He created him. Man could eat from any tree in the garden except one. When you hire people who can achieve their personal goals by doing what they're called to do and using their gifts and passions to do what they want to do and what your organization needs done, you can give them great freedom. It's like water flowing in the river. They just naturally fit and flow with the organization. I observed at HCA that when employees become dependent on their leaders to take action, it causes a great deal of frustration and anxiety. They don't feel the same sense of ownership and control of their lives as when they're given clear goals consistent with what they want to do and are empowered to act, knowing they have their leaders' support.

It's hard for people to be efficient if they spend too much time each day waiting for the leaders to give directions or make decisions for them. They feel drained when they spend too much time and energy waiting on decisions and instructions.

But when dependency on leaders is reduced, the team feels more empowered, more free, is more productive, and has higher morale because inidviduals sense a level of control and trust. They feel more like kids than adults when someone is always looking over their shoulders. People feel energized when they've had a productive day.

People don't always like being told what to do by their leaders, particularly people with personality profiles like mine.

Let's look at a simple example. Companies have expense reporting forms and guidelines for how to report expenses. This is uniform for all employees. They abide by policy with little complaint. If there were no policy and standard form and they were questioned individually by the managers, they would take that as looking over their shoulder and offensive. People thrive more readily with goals, guidelines, and procedures than with constant one-on-one oversight.

Organizations are sustained when people are empowered. If operations are based on the owners'/founders' being there, what happens when they are gone? What happens when they get sick? What happens when they are ready to retire? What happens when they die? The answer is obvious. The organization can't continue to function unless somebody like them takes over and carries on. Often in family businesses, this model of leadership is passed on to the children, who may not have the temperament or skill set to pull it off, and the business suffers. When the business suffers or fails, it can be really bad for employees. Good employees can work diligently for a long time and find themselves out of a job in small organizations with no "go forward" plan.

Summary

Let's review the benefits of operating like a franchise or large organization rather than a "mom and pop" operation. The first is being more efficient. It's hard for people to be efficient if they spend too much time each day waiting for the leaders to give directions or make decisions for them. Secondly, the team feels more empowered, more free, is more productive, and has higher morale because people feel like they have a level of control and trust. Last, but certainly not least, is the issue of leadership stability and succession planning. When everything revolves around the leaders, the organization shuts down and/or stops progress in the leaders' absence. Yet when there's a clear mission, a clear vision of the future, documented priorities, individual goals, clearly established accountability, and a wholesome set of values ingrained in the culture, the leaders can be absent for extended periods of time and the organization continues to progress.

Chapter 12 – The Approach To Power

When I came to understand how to empower people like a franchise operation, it changed my life as a leader for the better. I got more done in less time. By using this approach, I had a better handle on what was going on and knew in more detail how we were doing. I had more freedom day by day.

Application

I. On a scale of 1-10, how much do you lead through franchise-type techniques?

_____
_____
_____
_____

II. What changes do you need to make to empower people more?

_____
_____
_____
_____
_____
_____
_____

Chapter 13

EMPOWERMENT THROUGH EFFECTIVE DELEGATION

> **Thought:**
> How much better would your quality of work life be if you could delegate anything you do to people and be confident it would be done well?

"Moses' father-in-law said to him, 'The thing you're doing is not good. You will surely wear out, both yourself and these people who are with you, for the task is too heavy for you; you cannot do it alone.'"

Exodus 18:17-18

Empowering Progress

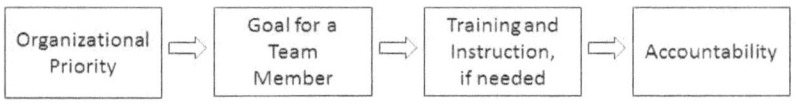

What's the first decision any leader has to make? You can only share power if you can delegate. There are two approaches we learn from Moses and Jethro, his father-in-law. Moses kept all of the work to himself, and people were gathered all around him looking for answers. Jethro's approach, that Moses later adopted, was to delegate to capable leaders and handle only the harder cases himself. In my experience, the three most important keys to effective delegation are:

- Be sure people understand the assignment.
- Be sure they know how to complete the assignment.
- Be sure they want the assignment.

Do They Understand?

It sounds so simple, doesn't it? You just tell people what to do. They are eager to please the boss, so they smile and nod. But that's where the breakdown often occurs. If you ask them whether they understand, they are likely to say yes whether they do or not. They don't want you to think they are unintelligent, and they are hoping they can figure it out.

Chapter 13 – Empowerment Through Effective Delegation

It has been my experience that the delegation process tends to break down in this very first step—communicating what you want people to do. Why is that? Because it's a complicated process.

It is not practical to explain everything people must do and how to do it. People need to understand the overall puzzle and where their part fits. They need to understand the overall objective to be achieved and the objective of their particular assignment.

The internal audit department at HCA was staffed with young, bright, hard-working professionals. They were very eager to please and very hesitant about saying they did not understand. They normally would smile and say they understood. If they didn't understand, they would wait until I left and hope a more experienced person on the team could explain it to them. After a few experiences, I learned to look deep into their eyes. I could discern either a look of comprehension or what I called a "dazed" or "glazed" look. When I saw this, I knew they did not understand. Sometimes I would say, "Tell me the first thing you will do to complete this assignment." Seldom did they know. Then I would go over it again and sometimes again until I was confident they understood what they were to do. If they can explain to you the objective of the job and a general approach for accomplishing it, they likely understand.

Do They Know How?

Sometimes people simply don't know how to do the task you are assigning. The answer to this is simple: either do it yourself, find someone who can, or train them.

Do They Want This Assignment?

Sometimes people know how to do something, but they simply don't have any interest in doing it—there's no passion.

When people complained about something in the organization, I tried to listen to what they thought should be changed or improved and assign them projects to fix the problem if I felt they had the competence. This did three things. First, it ensured the work was done by someone who cared about it. Second, it stopped a lot of complaining. Third, it reinforced a culture of not complaining about something unless you were willing to fix it. It's important for people to do work they believe in and care about.

Ecclesiastes says, "Whatever your hand finds to do, do it with all your might." This is an encouragement to work hard at whatever we do whether we like it or not. On a seemingly contradictory note, Jesus said, "My yoke is easy and my burden is light." Yet these two concepts complement one another when leaders give people work assignments for which they have the talent, experience, and passion rather than giving them assignments that feel like drudgery.

Chapter 13 – Empowerment Through Effective Delegation

DELEGATION PITFALLS

Delegation is important. Without it, you can't grow your staff and organization or increase your span of control. But there are some pitfalls to avoid. These pitfalls arise from ignoring several key teachings of Scripture:

- Know the condition of your flock. – Proverbs 27:23
- Don't lord it over them. – Matthew 20:20-28
- My yoke is easy and my burden is light. – Matthew 11:28-30
- Whoever forces you to go one mile, go with him two. – Matthew 5:41

Know the condition of your flock

This certainly applies to knowing the status of your organization or business. It also means to know what your people can handle. I have heard many leaders over the years describe what I consider a reckless approach to leadership. They say, "My approach is just throw them in over their heads in and let them sink or swim." The problem is sinking people tend to take others down with them, including the leader that threw them in.

I've seen the "throw them in over their heads approach" used many times. The "I" and "I"/"D" personalities are most prone to do this. When people are hired or existing people receive new assignments, often the leader gives a free reign and lets them go do it. You may say, "So what's wrong with that?" Well, you hire people believing they have a certain level of competence and motivation, but you've done absolutely nothing to validate or test it. The justification is, "They are professionals and I pay them well. Therefore, I just need to trust them." And certainly it's true that employees do need to feel like you have confidence in them. On the other extreme, some leaders are micromanagers who never really let go and give the employees autonomy.

It is also true their confidence is eroded and they get frustrated with micromanagers that never really let go and give them autonomy. So which approach is best?

Balanced Approach

In reality, you don't have to choose between throwing people in over their heads or looking over their shoulders all the time. There is a third alternative which will get the best results. It is a balanced approach. You give them freedom after you know what they can do. One way to know this is by verifying their prior work experience. The other is by observing them. Employees need to be fully immersed in meeting the objectives of the organization. They need to be part of an enterprise where they maintain their distinctiveness but contribute fully to the organization. This requires their being immersed in the job you have given them but not in over their heads. In this approach, you give them responsibility and authority incrementally.

I hired someone recently to do some work at my house. He had recently hired someone who said he had skills this contractor had never actually observed. He "threw him in over his head" and sent him to my house unsupervised. The person messed up the job.

Using this third alternative, you avoid a lot of mistakes and save a lot of time that would be spent correcting problems. Consider the example I just gave. It cost this contractor money to fix the problems caused by his employee. In addition, he risked not getting any future business from me, plus losing the potential referrals I would have given. This was a very costly mistake for the contractor that easily could have been avoided with some additional supervisory time of comparably minimal cost.

You should make the transition from supervision to independance as quickly as possible but not until you have a clear understanding of the capabilities of the new people. You can avoid any frustration the new employees may feel from being micromanaged by explaining your approach.

Chapter 13 – Empowerment Through Effective Delegation

That way, the employees know your intent is to let go but not throw them in over their heads. It's best to solicit the cooperation of the employees to make the transition as quickly as possible.

If you throw employees in over their heads, they're going to take on some water that isn't necessary. But when you walk them into the water up to their chins, they are fully immersed in the ownership of the project or task but not drowning. This is the optimal place for the employers and the employees to be.

The approach above is consistent with how Jesus led His disciples. First, He taught them. Then, He did things in their presence like healing people. Then, He sent them out in two's and had them come back and report on the results.

PERSONAL EXPERIENCE

In the last fifteen years of my career at HCA, I reported to thirteen different people. Therefore, I'm quite familiar with this process. I remember early in my career chafing over the engagement of my new manager. However, I noticed when new people reported to me, I insisted on a certain level of engagement. I went through the process just described.

I remember well reporting to a new manager and my CFO becoming extremely frustrated. He said, "Leon, we've been doing this for years and we know what we're doing. Why can't they just leave us alone?" I reminded him of the approach we both had used successfully over the years. I said, "We can make this process long and painful, or we can proactively engage with the new manager." The lights came on for the CFO and he said, "How quickly do you think we can do this?" I said, "If we really work at it, I think we can have him completely comfortable with us in the next thirty days. Then we will have substantial freedom just to go do our work." We worked hard at it, and in thirty days we were given a great deal of autonomy.

Don't lord it over them

Here, Scripture is telling us to avoid being abusive or overly controlling. People need and thrive on freedom when they are doing something they know how to do and for which they have a passion. When we are overly controlling, we limit people. We restrict their freedom, but we also restrict ours. It takes time and energy to look over someone's shoulder. When we don't empower people properly in the delegation process, we limit ourselves as well.

My yoke is easy and my burden is light

God never intended for people to be overloaded and burdened in their work. He doesn't intend for leaders to overburden people in their work either.

How many times do you find that people have more projects than they have time to complete? When this happens, they either put off one project and do the others or spread the time they have among all the projects. The result is that one project dies from neglect or all the projects suffer due to insufficient time and attention. The results can be devastating.

A better approach is to prioritize the projects. Are all equally time sensitive? Sometimes they are not. Are all equally important? Generally, they are not. Therefore, the leaders and employees should agree on which project gets deferred or dropped altogether. Otherwise, a high-priority project could die from neglect, or multiple important projects could be done poorly due to insufficient time and attention.

Don't overload your best people

> *"For six days, the Lord made the heavens and the earth, the sea and all that is in them, and rested on the seventh day; therefore the Lord blessed the Sabbath day and made it holy."*
>
> *Exodus 20:11*

Chapter 13 – Empowerment Through Effective Delegation

One application of this Scripture is that people should not be overloaded. This hurts individuals, but it also hurts the leaders. When leaders overload an employee or a group of employees, they position themselves to become overly dependent on an individual or a few individuals. The unintended consequences of ignoring this Scripture can be significant.

In organizations, delegation is sometimes like water. It follows the path of least resistance. Some people are eager to take on more and more work. But if you allow them to do so, you become overly dependent on them. This naturally tends to happen in small organizations but will also happen in larger ones if you are not careful.

I know of a businessman in Nashville who had a successful small business. He had one person responsible for his billing and accounts payable. That individual got sick. Customers were not being billed so his cash flow was cut off. Vendors were not being paid and were upset. It cost a substantial disruption in his business for a period of time. The fact was if it had continued, it could have ruined his business. I have seen a great many business owners, business leaders, and nonprofit leaders make this very statement about one or more members of their team.

One key rule of wise investing is diversification, i.e., don't put all your eggs in one basket. This applies to many aspects of organizational life, such as being overly dependent on one customer or supplier. It also applies to your people. Don't become overly dependent on a few key people. Mary, who I talk about next, is a real person that I had experience with, but I have changed the name. In fact, I have experienced more than on person like Mary.

It's not uncommon for leaders to brag on who they think are the very best people in the organization and the best fit for their jobs when, in fact, these people threaten the long-term success of the organization. This is counterintuitive, so we need to unpack it. Picture an employee that works hard, that does the work of two or three people, and that you count on enormously. Most leaders think everything is right about the situation. In fact, they say, "I don't know what I would do without Mary"—or whatever the key employee's name is. And that's the essence of the problem. What would you do without Mary?

Empowering Progress

The implication is quite simple. If something happens to Mary, you are in a real jam. But, you say, Mary isn't going anywhere. Does she never take vacation? Does she never get sick? Is she never going to retire? Is she not someday going to get promoted or transferred? If she's so good, is it not possible that someone would offer her a better package and hire her away from you? The reality is, it's not *if* you lose Mary, it's simply when and how. If you truly don't know what you would do without her, she is the most dangerous employee in your organization and you need to start figuring out now what you will do when she is gone.

Jesus' work was too important to not be passed on or have a backup plan when something happened to one of his followers. His plan was the one Paul shared with Timothy.

> *"The things which you heard from me in the presence of many witnesses, entrust these to faithful men who will be able to teach others also."*
>
> *2 Timothy 2:2*

There are some alternatives. You can hire someone else and split up the work. This is difficult, particularly in small organizations. Another alternative is to train one or more people on every task, like we did in internal audit. Then you have a backup when something happens to Mary. Again, this is hard in a small organization. Another alternative is to have a documentation file on how Mary does her job. We did this in internal audit due to the high turnover. Then at least someone can be trained using the documentation to fill the role more quickly.

Of course, the best solution is to plan and delegate in a way that avoids this problem from ever occurring. This is often easier said than done, especially in smaller organizations. Let's consider a typical scenario. The organization is having some success in its new business. Therefore, there is more work to do. Mary sees this as an opportunity to gain favor with the boss and have more impact and influence in the organization. Mary says,

Chapter 13 – Empowerment Through Effective Delegation

"I'll pick up the extra work." Mary does and the boss is very appreciative. This keeps happening, and the boss starts thinking about adding a person. Mary wants to gain favor with the boss to have influence in the organization and to provide more financially for her family. She says, "Don't hire anybody else. I will just work more and you can pay me more." That sounds like a good deal to the boss. So that is what the boss does. As this continues over time, Mary truly does become the person upon whom the organization is too dependent.

Other problems develop with Mary

Other than the fact Mary will eventually leave the organization, other problems might develop as well. Once Mary understands how important she is to the organization, she can make demands that may not be fair or reasonable to the leader or other employees. Mary can get inflexible, demanding, manipulative, and controlling. I've observed this many times when a leader gets overly dependent on one or a few people. What do you do? Your hands are tied, and you have let the rest of the organization down. In fact, you put the organization and the jobs of the other employees at risk. This does not bring balance and fairness to the workplace. It only jeopardizes it.

But, you say, Mary would never be that way. Maybe that's right. Maybe she is so dedicated to you and the organization that she would never behave inappropriately. But knowing you can't do without her, does she feel the freedom to take off when she truly is sick? Would she stay at work when she should be going to her kids' functions? Would she ignore the health of her marriage for the sake of the organization? Would she put the organization's needs ahead of her needs and her family's? If she does, is that right? Is that fair? If you allow that as the leader, have you blessed Mary? Have you blessed her family? Have you blessed her friends? Have you blessed her peers? Have you protected and blessed the organization? The obvious answer is no. So you see, sometimes a great, hard-working, loyal employee can be a risk to the organization and its long-term future.

My Experience with Marty

Let me tell you about Marty. This guy was a computer whiz. The company had an information technology department with hundreds of employees. I would ask them about the project for my department. They might say it would take six weeks. Marty could consistently do the project in two weeks. I was proud of Marty, bragged about Marty, and paid him well. I had begun to say, "I don't really know what I would do without him."

I realized I didn't know what I would do without Marty, but one day I would have to.

Then it dawned on me: someday somebody would see how good Marty really was, and that somebody would hire him away from me. Then what would I do? So we changed Marty's goals. Part of his goals was to write new programs. The other part of his goals related to documenting very well how to operate programs already written so that any programmer could come in and maintain, improve, or change those programs. This served us very well when this function grew. We hired someone else. They were able to carry on and even expand the base of what we already had developed very quickly because of the documentation and the crosstraining we had Marty do.

Nonprofit example

I am familiar with one rather large nonprofit ministry that had a multi-million-dollar budget. They had grown substantially and so had their computer infrastructure. They had one person in charge of all the tech-

Chapter 13 – Empowerment Through Effective Delegation

nology who did not like to document what he did and was not willing to train others. He made some mistakes that will have substantial negative effects on the organization for a long time. But the organization didn't feel it could correct, reprimand, or dismiss him for fear of losing him. In short, the leadership didn't think they could do without him.

Go the extra mile

Organizations need people who are willing to go the extra mile. Yet this need goes unmet when people do not agree with what needs to be done, or they do not know how to do the job. Think about it. If you don't believe something is a good plan for the organization, it is difficult to put your best effort into the work. If people are not qualified to do a particular project, exemplary effort is likewise difficult to muster.

In organizational life, it's nearly impossible to tell people everything they must do to complete complicated tasks. And even if you could, it would take too much time. So when you find people only doing what you tell them to do, it's time to probe some more. Ask questions to determine if they understand what you're assigning, if they simply don't have any interest in doing that work, or if they disagree with the objectives of the project. I can't overemphasize how critical it is that people be assigned work not only that they are capable of doing but that they want to do. In Revelation 3:20, Jesus says "Behold I stand at the door and knock. If any man will open it, I will come in and eat with him." Here is my thought: if the creator and master of the universe does not force Himself upon us, why do leaders think they should force their will on other people?

I remember one time asking a manager to schedule an audit at a hospital. He did not believe we should be doing that particular audit at that time. It takes some skill and effort to schedule an audit since people generally are not prepared and are not looking forward to one. Given that I knew his attitude, I should not have been surprised a few minutes later when he told me he just couldn't get it scheduled. In complex organizational structures, it's hard to get things done that you want to get done and nearly impossible to get things done you really don't care about doing or don't agree with.

So in the delegation process, watch out for people who are not going the extra mile. They may not have the talent to do the job or they may disagree with the plans.

Chapter 14

EMPOWERMENT THROUGH HIGH EXPECTATIONS

> **Thought:**
> Have you ever considered how much of your team's and organization's potential you are sacrificing because of your low expectations?

"Then Jesus said to his disciples,
'If anyone wishes to come after me,
he must deny himself, take up his cross, and follow me.'"

Matthew 16:24

> **Your expectations have a big influence on the team.**

Through the experience of having parents and being a parent, I know firsthand the impact of expectations. In my family, we were expected to work hard. We did, and it just seemed normal. In my wife's family, they did a lot of things to please and meet the expectations of other people. That thinking was so ingrained in her she still does it to this day. When I ask her why she's doing something, her response is often based on what somebody else expects. The expectations I had of my children impacted them significantly.

In society, I see the impact of expectations on people. There are for-profit businesses and nonprofit organizations that have cultures of high expectation. By contrast, there are those that have cultures of low expectation, resulting in mediocrity.

Sadly, I see this in the church in North America. Many churches have cultures of low expectation. Frankly, the standards to be involved in the social fraternity or sorority in college are higher than the membership standards of many churches.

The importance of teacher expectations in facilitating student learning has long been recognized.[11] What you believe about people drives your attitude toward them. Your attitude drives your communications with them and your behavior toward them. That in turn drives their attitude and behavior. They start reacting to you either positively or negatively. The first psychologist to systematically study this was a Harvard professor named Robert Rosenthal in an elementary school south of San Francisco.[12]

If you expect something to happen, you increase the chances of its happening. If you expect something good to happen, you tend to be optimistic, you look for opportunities, and you set goals. Over time, with this outlook of preparedness, chances greatly increase that something good will happen.

Conversely, when you expect something bad to happen, you are pessimistic, you miss opportunities, and you behave in a way that generally does bring some disappointment to your life. This is true even in the area of health. The medical field established long ago that people with positive and expectant attitudes are healthier and live longer than those with negative and depressed attitudes.

Similar research has been done with children. A study was done in inner-city schools with kids from economically depressed areas. One group of teachers was told they had students with below-average IQs. The other teachers were told their students had been tested and were gifted with very high IQs. At the end of several months, all the students were given standard achievement tests. As expected, the first set of children did poorly, and the other set of children scored very high on the achievement tests. The teachers were told afterward that all the students actually had average IQs.[13]

Poor students

So what was happening? The teachers who thought they had below-average students expected them to perform poorly. They never considered that their attitudes, actions, and follow-up could be the problem because they believed the students were destined to perform poorly. Think about what probably happened in these classrooms. The teachers likely did the minimum to inspire and encourage. I imagine the feedback was negative. Comments were likely made such as, "Will you pay attention?" "Are you ever going to learn this?" "Why can't you seem to get this right?" and "I give up. You'll never learn this."

Gifted Students

Now think about the feedback and interaction from the teachers who thought they were dealing with gifted students. The teachers expected the students to do well and probably assumed that if they didn't, it was their responsibility as the teachers. They worked harder themselves. They encouraged the students. The feedback was very different. They said things like "you can do it," "let me explain this a better way," "you didn't understand that because I did not do a good job of explaining it," and "let's spend some more time on this because I know you can get it."[14]

> **People tend to live up or down to your expectations.**

I could go on with examples, but I think you get the point. What the teachers expected not only drove their attitudes and behaviors, it had a significant impact on what the students were able to achieve.

> **I believed I had a great team at HCA.**
>
> **Some people disagreed with me. That didn't matter.**
>
> **What mattered most was that I believed it**
>
> **and my team believed it.**
>
> **That made the team better because *we believed* it.**

FRANK'S STORY

A young boy named Frank brought a Christmas present to school for his teacher Mrs. Jones. She opened all her gifts in front of the students. When she opened Frank's gift, the other kids laughed. It was a partially used bottle of perfume. Frank was obviously embarrassed because of the laughter, but Mrs. Jones thanked him for it and made over it like it was a fine gift even though she didn't quite understand.

Chapter 14 – Empowerment Through High Expectations

A bit later when none of the other students were around, Mrs. Jones asked Frank how he chose that particular gift. Tears came to his eyes as he explained it was his mom's perfume. He had given it to her the previous Christmas because he knew it was her favorite perfume. His mom was very sick that Christmas, but she always wore it and thanked Frank for it. She died a few months later. Frank told Mrs. Jones he hoped she liked it as much as his mom did and wanted her to have it so she would smell like his mom.

> *"Do not look out merely for your own interests.*
> *Look out for the interests of others."*
> *Philippians 2:4*

Mrs. Jones then took a special interest in Frank. She found out about his home life, which was tough. His father did the best he could but was poor and had to work long hours, leaving Frank to fend for himself. Mrs. Jones began to look at Frank differently. She determined she would encourage, support, and love him. In the final half of his fourth-grade year, Frank went from being a poor student to a very good student. Each year that followed, Frank went by and saw Mrs. Jones and told her how he was doing. Notably, he made A's every year. At some point, he moved away, and she didn't see him anymore.

A few years later, she got a note from Frank. He had just graduated from high school with honors and wanted to thank her for the difference she made it his life. Four years later, she got another note from Frank. He had just graduated from college at the top of his class. A few years later, she got another note thanking her for the impact she had on his life. He has just finished medical school and was now a doctor.

Leaders often underestimate the impact for both bad and good they can have on the lives of people in their spheres of influence. When we take a personal interest in people, understand their backgrounds and challenges, go the extra mile to meet some of their personal needs, and raise our expections of them, the impact can be deep. Often, it doesn't take anything heroic to make a big difference and a deep impression on someone's life.

I remember the going-away party the team threw for me when I left the internal audit department at HCA for a different role. A grown man stood with tears in his eyes, telling a story I had long since forgotten. I began to remember some of the details as he told the story. I was on vacation and made a call to a hospital CEO to recommend this fellow for a CFO position which he got. That move was a stepping stone to other career moves that turned out really well for him. I thought nothing of it and had long since forgotten. But because I took some time early in the morning while on vacation to help advance his career, it made a deep impression on him. It required very little of me. But it made a great difference to him.

Chapter 15

CONCLUSION

"Let all things be done decently and in order."
1 Corinthians 14:40 (KJV)

People need empowerment and freedom. They need to feel as though they own a piece of the organization's mission and vision. A key decision you must make is whether you're going to lead like Moses when he started out, with all the people gathered around him waiting for answers and direction, or like Jethro suggested, delegating to dependable people. In other words, are you going to run a "mom and pop" type operation, or are you going to lead it more like a franchise operation where you distribute power and authority to capable leaders?

On the family farm, I fed the calves. This was more involved than feeding the pigs because the milk had to be mixed properly and each calf had to be fed individually. Daddy taught me how to do it and entrusted me with it. If I had not done it well, the calves would not have grown, and Daddy would have inspected. But he had trained me well. I was conscientious about it, and I thoroughly enjoyed doing it. I felt like I owned a piece of the farm. I was empowered. Not only that, but Daddy gave me a piece of the profits. When we sold the calves, Daddy gave me the money from one of them. That really helped me feel like I owned a piece of the farm.

When you empower people properly, you give them great freedom, coupled with corresponding accountability. People feel like they own a piece of the organization because they have freedom to act and are compensated according to their contributions. The leader ensures there are policies and procedures to give guidance and direction without over-controlling. Operating manuals exist to illustrate best practices. Enabling control systems provide early warning signs when adjustments are needed. Training is provided when needed so team members feel competent and confident in their roles. People who are empowered properly have higher self-esteem, make more significant contributions to the organization, and are more committed to the long-term success of the organization.

PROGRESS

People need to know they are making progress. The first command God gave man was to be fruitful and multiply, which implies an expectation of progress. It is likewise implied in the parable of the talents, where the stewards were expected to multiply what the master gave them. God built within us the expectation and the need to make progress.

Empowering Progress

People followed Hitler because they believed he had solutions to their problems and could make their lives better. They started following him by choice. But after he got into power, they followed him by force. When you're in a position of leadership and authority over people's lives, the first choice you have to make is whether you are going to serve people. Will you have an influence and power that last, or are you going to assume the position of having the upper hand and control and manipulate people?

Chapter 15 – Conclusion

Power is the possibility to influence the actions of people.[15] In the context of Christian leadership, we want to influence other people positively for service of God's kingdom and for their own good. Having power is good if we use it to serve. We get real, lasting power—the ability to influence people—by serving them. Dale Carnegie once said, "You can have anything you want in life if you're willing to help enough other people get what they want." I have found this to be true. But I would add the purest form of service is driven by love of God and our fellow man, regardless of what comes back to us in return.

Power achieved or maintained by force is temporary power. People only respond to it as long as the threat remains. Since the key to continuing influence is service, it seems obvious that every leader, and especially every Christian leader, would serve. But it's not that simple. You have to have the heart to serve.

YOUR VIEW FROM THE ORGANIZATIONAL CHART

When you look at the organizational chart and your place in it, what do you see?

Most people see boxes connected by lines. Organizational charts are good. They bring needed structure and order to the organization. So please don't misunderstand some of the things I'm going to say next as suggesting otherwise. Nonetheless, if we view ourselves merely as "boxes," there are some things we need to remember:

- The box can begin to define us. It can limit us and the services we provide unnecessarily if we operate only within its perceived limits. If I had allowed my box on the organizational chart to define me, I would have had a hard time seeing myself as anything different than an internal auditor, since I spent so many years in that role with HCA. Alternately, if I had seen the role of Physician Services president as what defined me, I would never have had the freedom to do what I'm doing now.

Empowering Progress

- We can begin to relate to people through our boxes rather than our unique personalities. We may think we are more powerful, but we will be less unique and less human and, over time, much less effective in this approach.

- The boxes on organizational charts can be seen as sources of power and control. We can start depending on that box for influence.

- There is a real temptation when we view an organization from the postion of the box that we may start trying to control the other boxes.

At some point in my career, I chose a different view. In my mind, I knocked the sides and top out of the box and was left with only a platform for service. Viewing the organization this way gave me a sense of freedom. My view was that I was there to serve the organization and the people in it, and that I should be a good steward of any opportunity to serve. That view afforded me opportunities to lead multiple corporate functions at the same time. That view made it easier for me to transition from one role to another without letting the box define or limit me. But beware. When we serve well on our platforms, we need to be careful they don't become pedestals. According to Proverbs, pride precedes a fall (Proverbs 16:18). The higher the pedestal, the harder the fall.

I believe this principle is more important than most people understand. If the box starts to define you, it becomes your identity. When it becomes your identity, you become less than God created you to be. Work, although important, is not the totality of your life. Don't let your role on an organizational chart define your identity. If it does, when you no longer have the position, you've lost your sense of identity.

I can tell you firsthand that after spending many years leading internal audit, I had a great deal of my sense of identity wrapped up in that role. When I left Physician Services after twelve years, I realized a lot of my identity was tied to that role. When I left HCA after thirty-one years, I realized how much of my identity was tied to being an executive at HCA.

Chapter 15 – Conclusion

Anytime we let anything other than our identity in Christ define us, we are limiting the abundant life Christ gives us. Anytime we find our identity or security in anything or anyone other than God, we have formed an idol.

If you view your role in any organization as a platform for service, you will feel freer, serve more, serve better, and have more impact than if you see it as a box. The truth is, if you see your role as a box, it will make you less than who God created you to be. Conversely, if you see your role as a platform, you would tend to expand it.

In the movie *Cool Runnings*, John candy played the coach of a Jamaican bobsled team. Years earlier, his character had coached a team that won an Olympic gold medal. Later, he coached a team and cheated to win another medal. When his Jamaican team asked about it, his answer was predictable. He said, "After you win one, you feel like you just have to keep on winning to get the next one." Then, he said something along these lines: "But I realized if you're not enough without the medal, you will never be enough with the medal."

I don't look to John Candy or movies for my theology, but there was a lot of truth in that. If you don't feel special, and you're not enough without the position, will it be enough for you? I remember thinking that if I could just become assistant vice president, I would have arrived. Then I wanted to be vice president. Then I wanted to be senior vice president. God allowed me to have all that and more, but He helped me realize if His love for me and my identity in Christ weren't enough, no position would ever be enough. If you're not enough without the car, without the house, without the title or position, and without the money, you'll never be enough with it. If Jesus isn't enough for you, nothing the "world" offers you as a substitute will ever be enough for you either.

In one of the Indiana Jones movies, Harrison Ford's character was searching for the Holy Grail. Some bad guys were also searching for it, believing if they drank water from it, they would have "life eternal." After enduring many trials and tests, the final one was administered by an old knight who had lived seven hundred years guarding the grail. There were several cups on a table, and the grail seekers had to determine which one was the Holy

Grail. The bad guy got there first and chose a cup that belonged to a king. It was made out of pure gold. He poured water in and drank it. In a few seconds, his body disintegrated and he disappeared. The old knight said, "He chose poorly."

As Indiana Jones thought about the choice, he realized the cup of Christ would not have been like that of an earthly king, made of pure gold. He realized it would be the wooden cup representing humility and service. He drank out of the wooden cup, and his body didn't disintegrate. The old knight said, "You chose wisely."

Again, I don't look to the movies for my theology, but I did recognize truth in that movie. We have choices. We can follow what the world teaches about the importance of wealth, fame, and power, or we can believe what God says about humility, service, and sacrifice. Make no mistake about it: we make choices every day about which cup we will drink from. When we drink from the golden cup, our work will be judged, and it will be burned up, according to 1 Corinthians 3:13. But when we make the choice to drink from the cup of Christ, our works last and they will be rewarded in eternity, and we have life eternal.

It's your choice. Choose wisely!

Endnotes

Part I

#	Source	Page
1	Dan Miller, No More Dreaded Mondays (New York: Random House, 2009).	Page 7
2	Module 7: Organizational Direction, Vision, Mission, Goals, Objectives, McMonkey-McBean, page 2. Available from http://quizlet.com/11265967/module-7-organizational-direction-vision-mission-goals-objectives-flash-cards	Page 21
3	Dick Wells, 16 Stones (Franklin, TN: New Vantage Publishing Partners, 2012).	Page 30

Part II

#	Source	Page
1	Smallbusiness.chron.com, 5 Sources of Power in Organizations, by Paul Merchant, page 1-7. Available at http://smallbusiness.chron.com/5-sources-power-organizations-14467.html	Page 88
2	Google.com, Positional Power definition, page 1. Available from https://www.google.com/#q=positional+power+definition	Page 88
3	Jim Collins, Good to Great (New York: HarperCollins, 2001).	Page 89
4	Smallbusiness.chron.com, 5 Sources of Power in Organizations, by Paul Merchant, page 1-7. Available at http://smallbusiness.chron.com/5-sources-power-organizations-14467.html	Page 89
5	Google.com, Positional Power definition, page 1. Available from https://www.google.com/#q=positional+power+definition	Page 102
6	Ibid.	Page 102

7	Sources of Power, Article by Dr. Terry Stimson. The article identifies five sources of power—legitimate, coercive, and referent. It breaks power into two broad categories –positional and personal. Available from http://www.consultcli.com/Sourcespower.htm	Page 102
8	Blog.gaiam.com, Quotes by Robert Greenleaf, page 1. Available fromhttp://blog.gaiam.com/quotes/authors/robert-greenleaf	Page 103
9	Ibid.	Page 103
10	Note: I learned much and clarified much of my understanding about franchises through my discussions with Steve Lynn, former CEO of Sonic and Backyard Burgers.	Page 109
11	Teacher Expectations and Labeling, Article by Christine Rubie-Davies. Springer International Handbooks of Education, 2009, Volume 21, page 695-707. Available from http://link.springer.com/chapter/10.1007%2F978-0-387-73317-3_43#page-1	Page 134
12	Teachers' Expectations Can Influence How Students Perform, article by Alix Spiegel, September 17, 2012. Available from http://www.npr.org/blogs/health/2012/09/18/161159263/teachers-expectations-can-influence-how-students-perform	Page 134
13	Ibid.	Page 135
14	Ibid.	Page 136
15	Google.com, Positional Power definition, page 1.Available from https://www.google.com/#q=positional+power+definition	Page 141

Image Credits

Diana Rush–Organizational charts and graphics.
Clip art and photos are taken from Microsoft Word stock images, unless otherwise noted below or in the endnotes:

Page 39–Kettle–Jose Gelpi Diaz/DepositPhotos.com/©2014
Front Cover Design—Darrel Girardier/©2016

Enjoy additional books by Leon Drennan and Vision Leadership Foundation
Please visit www.vision-leadership.com

You can be a great leader, or a royal pain . . .

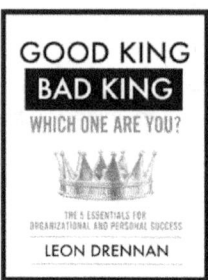

Good King/Bad King captures the essence of excellent leadership and reveals what it takes to live abundantly through five principles of visionary, profitable, and significant leadership. Whether you serve in a for-profit business, a church, nonprofit, or government, the blessing you bring to the people in your care and the organization you lead will make them grateful for your position in their lives. Let Leon Drennan's counsel and guidance show where you are on the path to leading with grace and skill, and inspire your noble pursuit of fine leadership.

Reap while you grow!

LIFE CAN OVERFLOW with the warmth and exuberance of spring or the lavish blessing of a late summer harvest. Other times, the bitter cold of loneliness, loss, or failure leaves you lifeless and desolate. Whatever the season, God can bring a harvest of blessing if you discover what He has for you in each. In *Seasons of the Soul*, Leon Drennan shows how to recognize which season you're experiencing and how to respond to God. If you cooperate with the Master Planner, you can even make the good seasons last longer and the bad seasons end sooner. God will never be one bit harder on you or provide one less miracle than you need. So dig in to this book, and reap a spiritual bounty—whatever your season.

Enjoy additional books by Leon Drennan and Vision Leadership Foundation
Please visit www.vision-leadership.com

Take a healthy view of the people you lead . . .

. . . AND THE PAIN YOU AVOID MAY BE YOUR OWN. Whether people are a boon or a bother really depends on you. On whether you help them feel like they count. On whether you make it clear where you're leading. And on whether you convince them that going there is what they want, too. You can be a great steward of an organization's resources only if you're a blessing to people. So assimilate the leadership know-how in this book, and establish the right perspective on the people you employ. Because the success of your company, organization, division, or department depends on *you*.

Do you feel like you're working harder than ever?

BUT NOT GETTING ANYWHERE personally or professionally? If so, author Leon Drennan can help. In The Power of Purpose and Priorities, he explains how to reassess your mission, values, and purpose in order to gain focus in your activities and develop priorities. Drennan says "less is more" when it comes to scheduling in business, family life, and social engagements. Wise people learn to prune away all nonessential activities in their personal lives and organizations to optimize the use of resources.. "You have to be clear about your purpose before you can set meaningful priorities for how you spend your time in this life," Drennan writes. "But more importantly, you have to be clear about your purpose and committed to it to have the endurance to see your priorities through. When you combine a clear understanding of your purpose with a few focused priorities, your life will have much greater impact."

Notes

Notes

Empowering Progress

www.ingramcontent.com/pod-product-compliance
Lightning Source LLC
Chambersburg PA
CBHW070619300426
44113CB00010B/1582